Improv(e):
Using Improv to Find Your Voice, Style, and Self

Jen Oleniczak Brown

BALBOA.
PRESS

A DIVISION OF HAY HOUSE

Balboa Press books may be ordered through booksellers or by contacting:

Balboa Press
A Division of Hay House
1663 Liberty Drive
Bloomington, IN 47403
www.balboapress.com
1 (877) 407-4847

Because of the dynamic nature of the Internet, any web addresses or
links contained in this book may have changed since publication and
may no longer be valid. The views expressed in this work are solely those
of the author and do not necessarily reflect the views of the publisher,
and the publisher hereby disclaims any responsibility for them.

The author of this book does not dispense medical advice or prescribe the use
of any technique as a form of treatment for physical, emotional, or medical
problems without the advice of a physician, either directly or indirectly. The
intent of the author is only to offer information of a general nature to help
you in your quest for emotional and spiritual well-being. In the event you use
any of the information in this book for yourself, which is your constitutional
right, the author and the publisher assume no responsibility for your actions.

Any people depicted in stock imagery provided by Thinkstock are models,
and such images are being used for illustrative purposes only.
Certain stock imagery © Thinkstock.

Print information available on the last page.

ISBN: 978-1-5043-9473-4 (sc)
ISBN: 978-1-5043-9472-7 (hc)
ISBN: 978-1-5043-9492-5 (e)

Library of Congress Control Number: 2017919599

Balboa Press rev. date: 01/03/2018

Contents

Who Cares?

You go into a public speaking situation. You've practiced in your head and you're really, really nervous. Or maybe just kind of nervous. Or maybe you know it's going to be bad. The last time you spoke in front of more than one other person, you flushed too much and felt so sweaty. Or maybe the last time you kept tripping over your words and you could tell people weren't listening to you. You think, this time it will be different. I won't sound like a robot. I practiced in my head, in the shower, in the car. I have this.

You go in. You do it.

And it doesn't turn out how you want it to turn out. You tripped over your words, you flushed, you got in your head and you didn't know what to say next. Or maybe it was just fine. It was nothing special, just another meeting, another pitch, another ok presentation.

And you think: *Maybe I'm not a good public speaker.*

Or maybe this is you: You get home. You're exhausted. Your family/ significant other/roommate says something to you and you are so tired from your day that you only half hear them, saying a quick 'Yeah ok' and really just focus on heading to a space where you don't have to see people anymore. Collapsing on your bed/couch/ floor, you finally relax from your day, just a little bit. Suddenly, your family/significant other/roommate is upset because they asked

1

you to do something and you SWEAR you never heard anything like that. They aren't crazy and you aren't crazy, you just missed the information. And maybe, this same situation just happened at work. With your boss. Or a client. Or a customer. And now you feel foolish.

And you think: *Maybe I'm not a good listener.*

Or maybe this is you: You go into a new situation, all ready to be yourself and wow them. They might be ready to hire, to do business, to date. You're dressed to impress. You get in there and something in your brain just stops. You end up being shy when you are actually quite bubbly, or you end up spewing word vomit everywhere. If it's an interview, you might be saying in your head 'STOP TALKING STOP TALKING STOP TALKING' or maybe it's the opposite – you have that witty/smart/incredible thing to say, and it doesn't come to you until you walk out the door. Another one bites the dust and you don't understand why you can't just be yourself. Maybe you don't know what it means to be you.

And you think: *Maybe I'm not good at being myself.*

All of these situations cause anxiety and uncertainty. I know because I've been in all of these situations. I coach students that have been there too. I work with professionals that experience this every day and continue to meet people that have that ME TOO moment when they hear that even the best speakers get nervous, even the best listeners miss things, and even the people that seem so unapologetically themselves get anxious sometimes. My business is built on the idea that people experience all of these things and want to improve. I know great ways that will help all of these situations get better. Ways that will build lasting skills and actionable things you can do while reading this book.

Before we start this adventure together, what are your expectations from this book? Why did you get it? Why was it given to you? Why did you find it somewhere and pick it up instead of regift it to your friend? Be clear and specific with your expectations before you dive in – even if it's 'my friend told me to read it' or 'you're my friend so I feel like I have to read it'. Just be sure to take a moment and think about what you want from this book.

You might like me and my advice, you might hate me and my advice. It's all good. Please know that like me or not, listen to me or not, try to keep an open mind until the end. After you've tried it, read it, gotten through it – then judge it. Improvisational comedy, or improv, is about being in the moment, paying attention to the here and now and responding to it. Chances are a lot of this might be new for you. You might not have experienced this type of thinking before, or tried these activities, or even thought about improv past SNL (which actually isn't improv!) New things are often a little uncomfortable. Embrace the discomfort.

Try it, and then make a choice.

Afterward, please judge. Send me an email, leave a review – whatever you like. I won't fight you on it or try to make you like me or my ideas, you won't get a nasty email back or some review arguing that this does work, as long as you judge it afterwards. Stay in the moment, try it out, and then decide.

Deal?

Now let's carry on.

Introduction: A Hostage Situation

I am a firm believer the playing field should be leveled as much as possible. So I want to level the playing field between you and me. I have a confession: I'm writing this book against my will and I'm holding my imposter syndrome hostage.

All joking aside, when I first considered the idea of writing a book, the thing that popped into my head was that little (loud) voice of self-doubt. You might know that voice as imposter syndrome or your inner critic or that undefined voice that says 'What do YOU have to offer?' Those six words kept ringing in my head.

A few years ago, I confronted that little voice head on and I lost. A publishing company reached out to me and asked if I would be interested in writing a book on improv. I was terrified and thrilled: terrified, see the above voice and six words. Thrilled: I love writing and I love inspiring people through improv. I run a company called The Engaging Educator (EE) that helps people improve their communication, presentation, and social skills through improv-based continuing education. I initially embraced the thrilled part and told my friend and business collaborator about the publishing company and offer, and the first thing he said was exactly what that ugly imposter syndrome voice was yelling: 'What do YOU have to offer? It's all been said.'

This led to a longer conversation about how he knew a guy who had all this incredible experience teaching at a corporate level, and he wrote a book on improv. It didn't do well. Why did this publisher want me to do it? At the time, I had only owned my business for about a year and a half, so I deferred to his experience and opinion. I let the idea slip away and found excuses not to do it. I stalled in writing; I was 'busy' and avoided calls and meetings. I just didn't do it. I let that voice of doubt win. The publishing company stopped emailing, and I was alone with my imposter syndrome. Not the best of company. The idea and opportunity passed.

Over the next four years, the idea of writing a book kept popping up. I kept ignoring it until finally I found myself asking why. Why wasn't I writing a book? I write for multiple outlets, I have a YouTube Channel, I tweet – why not put something more out there? This time, I didn't ask anyone and I acknowledged and trapped that much quieter and still present voice. This time, I made a choice to write it.

That voice will always be there – it's not gone, remember? I'm holding it hostage and I won't negotiate. Trust me, it gets out once in awhile. Every time it escapes, I step back, take note of how it got out, and trap it all over again. That voice is something I've come to acknowledge as natural – perhaps it's a primal urge to not overstretch or some subconscious effort to avoid embarrassment. Maybe it exists in myself and other Type A overachievers because we've always pushed past what's expected, and a push forward is generally greeted with a firm push back. Maybe it's because I'm a woman and to some extent I've always been told to be quieter and calm down, so I've created a monster in my head.

Guess what? I don't care why.

In the end, **why** I have imposter syndrome doesn't matter. What matters is I know how improv has helped the over 25,000 students, all non-actors, we've had with EE in just five years. I know I have something to share with more than the students who find our public classes or experience us through a private workshop.

And I know how the practice of improv and an improv mindset can help you find your voice, better your communication style and bring out your authentic and unapologetic self.

First, a bit of a backstory on how I got here and why you should give these ideas a shot. Through EE, a team of facilitators and I lead professional and personal development for everyone except actors. We work with corporations – Fortune 500 Companies to newly formed startups. We work with people who want to join these companies, leave them, interview for their first or next job. People that want to get raises, promotions, and new careers. We work with college graduates, senior executives, mid-level employees. We also work with schools and educators – doctoral programs to college students to pre-kindergarten students; individuals on the autism spectrum, verbal and non-verbal. We also work with people who want to better their interpersonal skills. Whether they signed up or their boss/teacher/co-worker/significant other signed them up, there is a desire to improve. We are a company that uses improv-based education to improve communication, presentation, and social skills.

Recently, we've started working with more women. Exponentially so. I never set out to be a woman-owned and operated company. I've hired (and fired) men (and women!), and one of my initial ex-major collaborators is a man. Within the past few years I've felt myself drawn to helping more women find their voices and boost their unapologetically awesome selves. At the same time, our demographic for public classes skewed strongly female – it's near a 2:1 ratio of women to men. Maybe it was the feeling of dread, depression and doubt I felt after the 2016 election or maybe it was what I was meant to do after finding my own voice. I do know that I quieted my imposter syndrome to make this book happen because of my desire to help more people, specifically women. I found MY best self through improv-based practice and thought, and I know with all of my heart and intuition that you can too. We get told all too often to quiet down, smile because you'll be prettier if you do, stop speaking up. What we need are ways to bring out our best selves, along with the confidence to be that self.

Guys, this doesn't mean if you're reading this book that you should put it down. We all need to improve. I've seen incredible progress from guys who want to develop listening and speaking skills. This isn't a women-only book – it has women-centric moments that can also be defined as 'anyone that has felt nervous or insecure' moments. So keep reading.

Improv is life – every single conversation, at its core, is improv. Think about it: you don't know what someone is going to say in response to what you say. You can't, and shouldn't, try to predict it. On top of conversation being about listening, responding and not predicting, every single person has to communicate, and should constantly be working on improving their communication style and skills. Even if you are sitting behind a computer all day, chances are you'll get into a situation that would have a better outcome if you had only listened better, or presented better, or even understood yourself and your audience more. Improv-based thinking and an improv mindset can relieve and lessen those 'if only' moments.

Disclosure: Reading this won't make you perfect. Any book or class that claims to fix you in one go is the same as the old-school snake oil salesman. Or better yet, the diet pill or workout that will make you beach body ready in 7 days or less. If I told you I knew a way to be bikini ready in one day, you'd politely nod and quietly think I was a scam artist. You can't take one class or read one book and be a better speaker. Your communication style and how you use improv to better it should be seen like a workout at the gym. You can't go once and expect to be fit and ready. You have to make it a practice as well as a lifestyle change. Think about this: if I asked you to put down this book and run 13 miles, right now, what would happen? I know I personally would fall over and die (or quit) because I'm not a runner. And even if you ARE a runner, you'd want to warm up or stretch, right? Look at improv as going to the gym for your brain. The first few times you go to the gym, it's awful. Painful, a chore, boring even, and then you find your groove, things start to feel good and it becomes part of your daily routine. Even when it is part of your routine, you still have to warm up before you run 13 miles. After you incorporate improv-based thinking and practice into your life, you'll still have to warm up before those big runs. This book is not meant to fix you. It's meant to give you ideas, tools and activities to start working out your brain, improve your communication style, and start the journey of becoming a better and stronger you.

User's Manual: The What and Why Behind Improv

Improv is largely unplanned with a strong structure of rules, ideas and guiding principles. It is generally created in the present moment and encompasses the idea of reacting and responding to things happening around you. Sounds like a basic conversation, right? It isn't about being crazy, witty, and funny. It's about listening and responding.

People tend to have a few conflicting opinions about improv.

They might love watching 'Whose Line is it Anyway?'

They might hate it because of a weird team building activity that made them quack like a duck for no particular reason or do a trust fall. (I would rather eat glass than lead or do a trust fall.)

They might feel they 'could never think that quickly' and would 'love to be that funny'.

They might have always wanted to take a class and didn't because they were too nervous or it was too expensive.

They might have taken a class and it's been a little weird and a little fun, but difficult to tie to life outside of class.

Of all the EE students I've connected with, most of them have some hot or cold reaction when they hear the word 'improv'. What do you think of when you hear the word improv? It can be negative – that's ok! It can be a good or bad vibe, and even after experiencing this book, you could still never want to take an improv class. Through this book I'll be explaining improv in a way that connects to a non-actor lifestyle, specifically to personal and professional life skills and self improvement. While some activities and examples have elements of creativity, making things up and 'playing pretend', they are written with a non-actor in mind. If you're trying to be onstage or on SNL then this probably isn't the right book for you. If you want to increase your skills at work, school, and in your relationships, career, and life, then this is the right book for you.

It's important to note that improv should be viewed as a heightened reality. Everything happens at a faster pace in improv: you don't talk about things, you do them. You don't talk about another person without them coming in at the exact moment you might not want them to. You can magic any prop you need, you can move time and space, you could be the king alien on a planet full of pineapples that are trying to destroy a planet full of Pad Thai. You can also be you, at work, finally telling your 'boss' what you really think of this new schedule and policy. You have to make decisions, otherwise the conversation stalls out – and the problem with a stalled out conversation in improv is you now have a class full of people watching you stall out. A little different than real life when you only have you, your inner critic and whoever you are conversing with to consider. With the heightened reality created by improv, everything happens faster, bigger and with more intensity. Sure, you probably aren't going to tell your boss off in real life. You might experiment with ways of doing it, or just blowing off steam by losing it, or seeing what might happen if you just told another individual to take their ideas and shove it.

Best part?

All of it ends in just a few minutes, and there are no repercussions. We teach short-form improv with EE. Sparing you the improv pedagogy, short-form involves quick, snappy moments that usually end in three to five minutes. They encourage the development of skills because you have to make choices and you have to make them fast. There are also no repercussions to worry about because everyone in the class is working on something – so if for one conversation you end up being someone's boss that gets yelled at for being awful and in the next, someone else is your fiancé that needs to take out the trash more often, it's all even at the end. Plus, you might never see these people again in your life. You can play as hard as you want, all ends up forgotten and forgiven except for the skills you learn along the way.

Improv-based thinking, for those of you not breaking down walls to get to your local improv class, really connects with how we teach our classes: you need to make specific choices, you need to be aware and present, you need to make things happen, you need to play, you need to fail and you need to reflect on what just happened. Simple stuff, right? Good thing EE's approach to improv is scaffolded. You master the 'easy' stuff before you hit the 'hard' stuff. Just keep in mind, some things might be easier than others – you might struggle with something that seems easy, and cruise through something that seems difficult. Take it moment by moment, and be present, reflect and try again.

This book and its information come with one more disclosure: some of these activities and ideas might be different than what you are used to. They might seem odd, silly or uncomfortable. To this, my go-to advice is two-fold and always the same. The first part is what a mentor told me years ago when I told her I was uncomfortable with the career change that was inevitably happening in my life: Life begins at the edge of your comfort zone. Discomfort isn't always pleasant – we *do* learn a lot when we are uncomfortable. Sometimes it's as simple as how we can avoid that uncomfortable situation again! Other times it's deeper and longer lasting than avoidance. We figure out life while we are uncomfortable. It moves us from being stagnant and safe, and forces us to make changes. The other bit of advice I have regarding the potential silliness and discomfort with some of the suggestions in this book is what we agreed upon earlier. And you made a deal when you kept reading! Try it, see what happens, and then judge it afterward. You might like it or you might hate it. Judge it when it's over and you've given it a fair chance. Remember, improv is all about being present. You don't think about your dinner or tomorrow or your date next week; you are 100% in the here and now. Read this book and consider the lessons it contains in the present moment, judging it after you've reflected. Afterward, and by all means, call me, email me, Amazon review me – whatever! While you're in the book, try it on and just pay attention to how you feel. You never know – it might be magic.

Deal for real this time?

Reflection and Growth

Throughout this book, there are several opportunities to reflect on the activities. Reflection is one of the big ideas that we at EE are committed to. We value, encourage and believe in the idea that you have to think about what you just experienced in order to grow. During class, after exercises and between programs, we encourage students to answer the question of 'So What?' Many other improv companies focus more on performance and the 'fun' part of what they are doing – we are thinking about how all of this connects to real life. While our improv is a lot of fun, there is always something more than laughter and enjoyment to be gotten through our activities.

I encourage reflection, both while you are reading, before and after activities and even during everyday moments that remind you of something in this book – or things in this book that remind you of everyday moments! Write all over it – in the margins, on the covers, over some of the words, and reflect on what you think and how you feel. Ask yourself So What and figure out what just happened or how you reacted or how this connects to your expectations and every day life. If you aren't a writer, then scribble, draw, build a castle – anything to get you thinking about what just happened! After you've answered the So What, think about 'Now What'. If you read something that makes you want to take action or think differently, improve in some way or change how you connect in situations, think about your Now What. Make a plan and set a goal.

I've split this book into three major sections: Finding Your Voice, Finding Your Communication Style, and Finding Yourself. In each section, you'll find activities and thought prompt areas called 'Try This'. I encourage you to do exactly that: try them and reflect on the experience. All of them can be 'tried' multiple times to different results each time, and a lot of them are great for tracking progress and growth. The idea of practice and repetition cannot be stressed enough. It almost seems counterintuitive, no? Practice improv? The truth is, improv is less about the spontaneous and more about a mindset around what happens in a moment. There are specific ideas and rules that happen when it's being done 'right'. Remember, right isn't necessarily funny; it's actively listening, being present and connected to what's happening around you, without preconceived notions and agendas. When improv is done right, failure doesn't exist. Everything is growth and you fail forward, always picking something up on your way down. You have control over what happens because you are making choices based on what is happening around you, because you are paying attention to it at a level you weren't before. And that fear of the unknown? You follow it.

END OF USER MANUAL

Finding Your Voice

People tend to fall in one of three camps when it comes to public speaking: folks that fear and hate it to some degree, folks that feel comfortable when they can prep and hate impromptu speaking, and folks that enjoy it and want to get better. If you don't readily identify with one of these three categories, take a moment and assess how you feel about public speaking.

If you don't fall into one of those three categories and think you are the best public speaker ever and need zero improvements, please make your way to the Finding Yourself section of this book and be sure your self-awareness is in check.

PUBLIC SPEAKING isn't just this all caps and flashing lights formal presentation to hundreds of people. I'm talking about anything more than chatting with your family and friends. A conversation with one person constitutes a conversation with an audience. Everyone should strive to be a better speaker and communicator, and everyone should think they could benefit from improvement. Stagnancy isn't effective – it's where things go to die.

If you DO hate public speaking to some degree, you are not alone. The truth? Most people fear public speaking more than they fear death. Just recently I saw an article stating that the only thing people feared more than public speaking was reptiles.

Reptiles.

Fears of Godzilla aside, most people have some level of anxiety with public speaking because of situations in the past that had a negative outcome. Whether that's something like intense sweating, flushing or anxiety, a mortifying mistake or *that look* on the audience's faces that screams 'I am so bored!', public speaking as a whole doesn't get a great rap. Presenting is <u>slightly</u> different since most people consider a presentation 'prepared' public speaking, and tend to be a bit more comfortable after what they deem 'enough prep'. And when that prep fails them? The common reaction: 'I'm just not a good public speaker.'

I challenge that reaction. Anyone can be a good public speaker <u>if they try</u>. Again, let's think about the connection with physical activity. Put this book down and go run 13 miles.

No?

Why not?

Because you'd pass out. As mentioned earlier, even if you've been training for a marathon or consider yourself a runner, you'd want to warm up. And if you haven't been training for a marathon and you are not a runner, you'd need to prepare for something like that. Why do we view speaking any differently? Depending on the source, you use 70-100 muscles just to say ONE word. The average person speaks at a rate of 125-150 words per minute. A five-minute speech? That's 625 – 750 words.

You use your muscles A LOT to speak.

So why do we view speaking as a talent and exercising to be fit as a fact of life? It's flawed thinking. Why shouldn't we be expected to warm up our speaking muscles in the same way we have to warm up our leg muscles? Why shouldn't we practice and do cardio for our speaking skills in the same way we do cardio for our hearts? It's about training your muscles.

If you easily identify with one of the three above categories – fear and hate it; like some of it, hate some of it; like it and want to get better – there are ways to develop these skills through improv-based activities. Most people tend to worry about WHAT they are going to say instead of HOW they are going to say it. Truth be told, the 'how' is just as important, if not more so, than the 'what'. You could tell a group of people how to immediately get one million dollars and if you do it in a boring and lifeless manner, packed with filler words and sound as if you are reading off a page, people will forget what you have to say, or worse, stop paying attention. On the flip side, you could tell a group of people a recipe for banana bread and if you do it in an interesting and passionate manner, staying specific and on point, everyone will be excited about banana bread. Quite a bit lies in the delivery.

There are a few basic things that help when it comes to polishing speaking skills that apply to everyone in every situation. These provide a foundation that's necessary before digging into the personalized improv-heavy improvement. If there isn't a strong base before you start adjusting and growing skills like pivoting, flexibility, creativity and the 'it' factor, everything falls apart. Before you even start to think about your audience, or anything else for that matter, you have to do a step that many people miss between figuring out what they're going to say and saying it. You have to warm up.

Warming Up

In case you missed the first fifty times I've likened communication skills to exercise habits, here's a whole section dedicated to seeing that metaphor through!

First, self-assessment time.

Think of the last meeting, speech, or important conversation you had. Answer the following questions:

Did you warm up your voice?

Did you practice? How much?

You probably didn't warm up enough before you spoke (if you did, nice job) and you practiced either in your head, not actually saying the words out loud, or not nearly enough. I often ask new clients how their last public speaking situation went and the answers range from 'fine' to 'terrible' to 'not as good as I wanted'. Then I ask them how much they warmed up or practiced. Their response? Usually a sheepish, 'I went over it in my head in the car/subway/train to the office' or a simple 'no'. Even if you did practice and knew it like the back of your hand at your home, you might have made a mistake once you got to your office. Those are some of the most frustrating mistakes – you are 100% sure you have this down perfectly, and suddenly, for some weird reason, you lose it all midway through.

Your presentation and speaking skills all start with you warming up your voice. And I'm not talking about a cup of coffee or tea before you speak. I'm talking about stretching those muscles and getting ready to run those miles. Good warm ups over-stretch muscles just a bit to get them ready for the workout. The same goes for vocal warm ups. You push until you can feel the stretch.

Try This

Do you trip over your words? I find that even great speakers get tongue-tied. The reason lies somewhere between our mouths working faster than our brains and our mouth muscles failing to keep up. One of the simplest ways to stretch these muscles is to do tongue twisters.

Before you start pulling out the tongue-twisters you did in grade school to 'accidentally' swear, the point of a tongue-twister in this regard is to say the phrase as slowly and as deliberately as possible. Make sure to over-enunciate each word; you should feel like you are working out your jaw, lips, and tongue. You should also feel like you are just about to spit while saying a tongue twister. It's also ok if you DO spit. This isn't to say that you would ever talk like this in real life – you are stretching the muscles in an elevated way to get them *ready* for real life – heightened reality, remember?

With those points in mind, here are some tongue-twisters that warm up your mouth:

Red leather, yellow leather
Irish wristwatch
The lips the teeth the tip of the tongue the tip of the tongue the teeth the lips
The sixth sick sheik's sixth sheep's sick*

*According to The Guinness Book of World Records, this is the toughest tongue twister on record. How they measure that is beyond me. This one is HARD.

While not all tongue twisters are created equal, most, if not all, will do a great job. The key is to say each at least three times in that slow and deliberate manner. It is also important to <u>think</u> about the words that are coming out of your mouth and over-emphasize each consonant and vowel. They are all fairly simple if you think about the words and their meaning, and always keep in mind this is not about saying them as quickly as possible. It's about using the different areas of your mouth as much as possible. The over-enunciation warms up your mouth muscles. Thinking carefully about the words that are coming out of your mouth slows down and solidifies the connection between your brain and your mouth. When you trip over words, or use a lot of filler words, you're running your mouth at a different speed than your brain, which causes you to get tongue-tied. Slowing down to properly say the tongue twisters will bring that timing a bit closer, and help you connect your thoughts. And shouldn't we be thinking about the words that are coming out of our mouths instead of just running our mouths?

Try This

Are you soft-spoken? Do you sound breathy when you talk? Do you get nervous? Before you speak, take a deep breath for yourself. Be sure your feet are underneath your knees, which should be underneath your hips, which should be underneath your shoulders. Your pose and stance while speaking effects how you feel and how your audience perceives you. Don't stand with one hip jutted out or one leg crossed in front of the other – aside from looking sloppy and overly casual, you're telegraphing nervousness and unprofessionalism. If you're really nervous, try Amy Cuddy's Power Pose. Stand with your hands on your hips for 90 seconds in a Wonder Woman or superhero stance. You will be infused with confidence. There has been a bit of debate regarding the science behind this – I do think it helps with confidence and pose. Try it and tell me you don't feel a little more bad ass.

If you are sitting while you are speaking, be sure you have both feet on the ground. If you are wearing a dress or a skirt, really try to connect with the floor as much as possible. Be careful if you are crossing your legs – you don't want to cling to that tension or have a place for it to go by clenching! For both sitting and standing, you want to unclench your butt. To see what I'm specifically referring to, clench your butt and say 'Hello'. Now unclench your butt and say 'Hello'. Feel and hear the difference? We carry tension in all different areas of our body, and many people carry it in their lower half, which will impede proper breath support. Many women, myself included, also carry tension in the shoulder and neck region. A nice way to relieve this is to pull your shoulders all the way up to your ears and hold them there. Keep breathing and after a few moments, drop them back down. This feels FANTASTIC when you've been at a computer all day, so try it whenever you start to feel your shoulders creeping on up to hang out with your ears.

After you've adjusted how you stand and sit, and taken that big breath, make sure you are breathing enough while you're speaking. If you are taking big, gaspy breaths mid-sentence, you might not be breathing when you should. Take advantage of punctuation; breathing at a period, comma, or semi-colon allows a pause and breath. This is also a great way to really think about the words that are coming out of your mouth, as you have to think of them as actual sentences instead of free-flowing word vomit.

This next part of our breathing warm up should be done in the privacy of your own space, unless you want to have a co-worker or friend come running. If you feel soft spoken, or have been told that you are, one of the best ways to become louder is to practice being louder in a very contrived manner. Count from one to ten, one being the softest and ten being a throat-pulling yell. Your normal speaking volume shouldn't be a yell or a whisper, and this activity will show you what too much or too little feels like. If you don't know your limits, how will you ever know what loud enough is? Quick thought: ladies, when we get TOO loud, we get into a pitchy head voice. It's that place where we get shrill – I'm guilty of this too. When you are doing this activity, use that head voice for the 'too loud' part of the exercise. Take note of the volume that feels like it's coming from the top of your head. That's your shrill volume. Avoid it. It's not only unpleasant for everyone to listen to, it's not healthy for your voice. After you've practiced with the extremes, find a volume that you feel comfortable with between five and eight. This is usually the best speaking volume for most people, especially if you are soft-spoken. If your audience can't hear you, why should they care?

Volume and vocal power are connected to your breath support. One way to build breath support involves a form of stretching. Place one hand on your stomach and one hand on your back. Take a deep breath in, really thinking about filling up your hands with air, and letting your stomach contract when you breathe out. Now, take one deep breath in and count out audibly at a fairly quick pace, with your volume at a five to eight. You are counting on the exhale, and stop counting when you run out of air. Remember the number you ended on, and do the same thing again tomorrow, and the next day, and whenever you can remember to do this activity. Aside from some beautiful relaxation with this deep breathing, it's a great way to increase your lung capacity. Your number should go up the more you do it.

Try This

While this section has been devoted to non-improv activities, there is a tip that directly connects to an improv idea that I'd like to share: fake it until you make it.

Think about how you stand when you are speaking to another person. Maybe that's a friend, family member, or coworker. If it's a nice, calm and friendly conversation, you probably aren't tensing up a lot. What happens when someone says something that stresses you out? Or the situation suddenly becomes tense? Or you are interviewing for a job and you get nervous?

Think about where you might hold that nervousness. Is it in your butt? Your shoulders? Your back? Wherever you hold that nervous energy, the people you are talking to can feel it. We telegraph emotions, both verbally and non-verbally. If you see someone speaking and they look incredibly awkward and nervous, you're going to feel awkward and nervous for them. And you'll remember how awkward and nervous it was to watch them speak. You don't want to be that person.

How does this tie into 'fake it until you make it'? You can practice an open, welcoming stance at home in front of your mirror, and then continue to use that stance and fall back into it when necessary. Even when you get nervous, you can adjust your body back to this stance and you'll trick your brain – and the people you are talking to – into thinking you are more relaxed than you actually are.

What is an open, welcoming stance, and how can we get there? While you don't have to use a mirror for this activity; it is nice to see WHAT you look like when you are standing in an open and welcoming manner! An Alexander Roll is a simple and daily (or whenever you have time) activity to center and connect back into that calm and open stance. Before you do the activity, read this entire paragraph so you understand how to do the activity first, and be sure to breathe the whole time! Start by standing with your feet flat on the floor, your feet under your knees, your knees under your hips, your hips under your shoulders. Don't lock your knees, and stand as if someone has tied a balloon to the top of your head, and it's holding you up tall and straight. Now, someone snips the balloon and your chin falls to your chest. Slowly start rolling down as if you were headed to touch your toes – the point is not to reach down to touch your toes, the point is to hang over comfortably. Make sure your knees aren't locked, your neck isn't tense and just hang, taking deep breaths in and out. Let some sound out on a breath – maybe an 'ahhh' or 'haaa'. Now, start to roll back up, as if you were stacking the bones of your back one by one on top of each other, letting your head come up last.

Try it and see how you feel.

Most students, after they try this activity, fall in love with it. An actor named Frederick Matthias Alexander created this practice over 100 years ago. Alexander was a great Shakespearian actor that found he frequently lost his voice. After numerous doctor trips, with nothing medically wrong with his voice, he discovered the problem – and solved it – by adjusting his posture and addressing his tension.

Today, Alexander Technique is taught by skilled and licensed teachers all over the world – it's a fascinating practice, and I highly recommend looking into it if you want to work through tension in your body. I had one student, a few years ago, with chronic back pain. She was coming to me from a law firm where she was the lone female in the office, and felt she wasn't getting enough credit from her coworkers. We were working on her confidence in speaking up at meetings as well as her presentation style. I suggested during one session that she start doing an Alexander Roll, a component of Alexander Technique, in the morning before work to find her center and relax. She had already been using yoga for her back pain, and this was similar enough for her to 'buy in'. A few months and coaching sessions pass, and I get an email from her about her back pain – she told me she had been doing the roll every morning for the last two months, and her back pain improved tremendously. And her firm? She was finally speaking up and getting noticed.

The Alexander Technique isn't a cure all and like everything, it won't be for everyone. It's a really simple thing to try for a few weeks to see what it does – and if anything, we all need a little time to just breathe for ourselves every once in awhile.

Warming up not only helps with performance, it also helps with nervousness. By warming up, you take time to find your center and calm. We often get in our own way because of nerves or discomfort. As adults, we make rules for ourselves and set up unreasonable and unclear expectations and when we don't meet those expectations or we break those rules, we are disappointed. Then the next time the same or a similar situation comes up, we start to fear that feeling of disappointment and missed expectations, hence the nervousness. The unknown is scary and we can get past it by preparing as much as possible.

Flexibility + Pivoting

Pivoting and flexibility are skills, not gifts. Moving and switching gears in the moment can be taught and learned. They are required in impromptu speaking, since careful listening AND flexibility are the keys to successful 'in the moment communication'. Improv and improv based thinking work both of these skills to exhaustion, and while many people think that improv is all about being spontaneous, flexibility has a stronger presence.

Recently, I was at an event where I was chatting with a self-proclaimed 'good-speaker'. She told me that she loved to speak in public and had no problem with prepared presentations. The problem, she said, occurred in those moments where she was asked at the last minute to give remarks or say a few words before a planned event. Apparently she froze, got tongue tied and felt extremely foolish. Impromptu speaking just wasn't her thing, she said, and it never would be. 'I'm just not good at it!'

Sound familiar?

The problem isn't her (your) speaking skills; it was her (your) lack of flexibility and listening in those impromptu moments. Her 'few remarks' task wasn't that hard – she had to think about what had just happened and what was about to happen, and comment on it. To her, the unplanned element of it was terrifying. When we broke it down to a simple task, she had a hard time believing it was just that easy. The thing is – it IS that easy.

Flexibility and the ability to pivot are all about relinquishing control and having a comfort in the unknown. In order to be flexible, you have to dismiss your own agenda (control), embrace being present (control and comfort in the unknown), and not think about negative associations you might have with impromptu speaking (comfort in the unknown). You focus on responding and reacting to the moment at hand, paying attention to what is happening around you, and dismiss everything else.

Simple right? It is once you break it down improv-style.

I think people who haven't taken an improv class before think it's a crew of crazy people who live every single moment by the seat of their pants and are the most flexible people on the planet. Sure, there are some people in improv that fit that mold. There are also some accountants and entrepreneurs and teachers and writers who do as well. People are people and everyone is different. If you have problems with flexibility and pivoting in the moment, look around. If you're in a room with another person, chances are they might have some issues with flexibility and pivoting too.

One of the first and easiest things you can do is actively practice responding in the moment, and stop thinking about everything else. Just listen to what is being asked of you and respond to it.

This is <u>hard</u>. We want to be a few steps ahead and don't usually like surprises. It stands to repeat, again: focus on the moment in front of you. Dismiss your thoughts on dinner, dating, that weird noise you keep hearing – just listen to the person and situation in front of you. Now, think about the potential responses to the moment in front of you. You could respond like every day – that's generally the immediate response that pops into your head, unless you've had an amazing or terrible day. You could also respond in a way that changes the dynamic of the situation. You could also respond in a way that blows the situation up – in improv thinking, I like to tell students, 'think about your bomb drop.' What's the one thing you could say in a situation that would make everything change? Now what's the one thing you could say in a situation that would be a little out of character, and not quite bomb-drop category? Maybe you are always incredibly compromising…not this time! Or maybe you are always argumentative…compromise this time!

This activity isn't meant to change who you are. It's meant for you to start thinking about different outcomes. After you've assessed a few possible responses that you could give, now think of the outcomes the other person could give. Do at least three possibilities: the everyday response, the bomb drop, and the one in between the two. Thinking about possibilities is a simple way to start preparing for the unexpected.

Be careful with this activity: I've personally found if I start thinking about too many options, I find myself not paying attention in the moment. Be sure that you are still paying attention to the moment at hand and responding in real time. It's a balancing act that becomes easier in time. And it's not fool proof – there are still times that responses leave me speechless! If you find yourself overanalyzing or overthinking, stop and check in with yourself. If you aren't paying attention, start!

Actively putting yourself in a variety of different situations is another way you can learn flexibility. There are some situations that require flexibility – without it, the conversation and moment stagnates. That's often easier said than done – why make a mistake and try flexibility for the first time in an important situation when you could attempt to plan out every moment and every interaction? Lucky for everyone that's ever heard 'just relax' and 'go with the flow' and gotten annoyed, there are ways to work on your flexibility. Think of a normal, every day conversation. You generally don't consciously enter a conversation knowing exactly how it's going to go. You should listen, pay attention, and respond to what's placed in front of you. Unfortunately, a lot of the time we try to focus on our own agenda in conversations and communication. Flexibility is best practiced while existing in the present moment and eliminating those moments of half-attention and half-focus. You listen, you digest, and you react to what's in front of you. You might be thinking: Wait, that's not flexibility, that's just listening!

Yep.

Flexibility is a bit of an illusion. I think the most flexible people are actually the best listeners. If a person is truly in the moment, they can be perceived as flexible, because all they are doing is listening and responding to that moment. Think about your own flexibility. Why aren't you as flexible as you want to be? Is it because you get an idea in your head that you love so much and you don't want to get rid of it? Is it because once you get a plan, you don't want to deviate? Is it because you are only focused on your own path? There's a possibility that you might have said yes to any one of those questions – and that's the easy kind of flexibility to work on. Sure, you might also have some control and Type A issues (ahem, me too) and eventually, you'll need to work on those. If you simply need to work on your presence in the current moment, you're in luck. It's an easy-ish fix, chock full of activities that you can immediately start doing.

Try This

Have an open conversation with someone and let it naturally flow. Don't create or come in with a specific purpose for the conversation; just follow the dialogue as it goes down the rabbit hole. Feel free to be transparent with the person you're talking to, and tell them you just want to practice 'going with the flow' and follow the momentum of the conversation. Check in with yourself every once in awhile – are you driving the conversation? Are you trying to direct it somewhere? If you are, stop. Just follow along! Don't try to accomplish anything aside from a simple, natural conversation. You can also use a variation of the improv activity 'Last Word'. The idea behind last word is simple: in a conversation, the last word of one person becomes the first word of another person. For example:

Person A: I think it's a lovely day!
Person B: Day like this, I'm headed to the beach!

It gives the conversation momentum, an element of fun, and you HAVE to listen. I highly recommend letting someone know you are doing this before they start wondering why you sound like Yoda.

Try This

Take one day this week to go along with everything that gets presented to you (within reason). Have that single day be your 'go with the flow' day, and follow someone else's lead. If someone suggests you quit your job or get married, think about it first – I'm referring to simple ideas and decisions. Maybe that means being transparent with someone close to you, or just quietly going along with everything that gets suggested and deferring decisions to someone else. If this already sounds like you, then do the opposite and make choices today and don't follow anyone's lead. If a full day is too much, try a half-day or even just a few hours. The point is to move away from your norm. You're trying to shake things up. If you are like most people and do a bit of both, follow along one day and make strong choices another. No matter how difficult it is, be different from your usual day to day and stick with it as much as possible. Change always feels difficult and those difficult moments are the ones where we learn the most. Afterward, be sure to reflect on how you felt with the change, what worked and what didn't.

As mentioned before, practicing these activities improves a certain type of flexibility, the kind that is about being in and open to the present. The other issue with flexibility is related to our ideas of control. Some people just want things to go in a specific way, and if that way is disrupted, the result is anxiety. This is completely normal. Sometimes, you just need to repeat those words to yourself: My anxiety is normal. The thing is, it isn't fun. I know first hand how crippling anxiety can be – I had my first world-ending panic attack when I was transitioning from being a camp teacher and theatre person to the museum world. Things just weren't going the way I wanted and I felt lost, so everything felt like a disaster. Control issues are another aspect of life that can be helped through improv. By going along with the moment and being aware of how you feel about your lack or abundance of control, you can practice either consciously giving it up or taking it. Start to identify the situations where you need control in order to feel calm. While I don't teach or use trust falls (I would rather eat glass) I am a big fan of trust walks. Find a friend who is feeling adventurous and stand face to face. Put Put your hands up in front of you and connect fingertips with your friend. Now, one of you should close their eyes and the other will lead that person around by only the touch of fingertips. No talking or laughing – if you do, that person will follow the noise, which isn't the activity. There are two important things to remember: Don't let the other person crash into something and be sure that if your eyes are closed, you are always walking forward. The person with their eyes open should be walking backwards, because they can see!

This activity really assesses how you handle control. You're either giving it up by letting someone be responsible for your safety and well being while you literally can't see where you are going, or you are taking on the safety and well being of another person by being their eyes. Think about what role you preferred and why you preferred it. If you liked having your eyes closed, maybe you like giving up control because you always have it. Or maybe you liked it because you go with the flow – or maybe you hated it because you couldn't tell where you were going. Or you were nervous and shaking the whole time. Really think about how you felt in each role, and connect that to how you feel with your flexibility style.

Flexibility can't be improved in a single day. It's often a conscious choice and these skills are developed with practice. How often have you heard 'just roll with it'? I even wrote it into the last two activities and cringed a bit, because it's not something that can change in a moment nor is it easy. It's a choice to build a threshold for flexibility and also a forgiveness of failure if the outcome isn't what you wanted it to be. Going along with the moment might end up not working out the first or fifth time – it might work the second, third and fourth time. You have to keep doing it in order to grow. Building the skill of flexibility and the ability to follow when necessary will take time, so do not get discouraged if it takes longer than you expected.

Pivoting is another subject entirely. Flexibility might be defined as going with the flow, while pivoting is going with the flow and keeping your end goal firmly in sight, changing strategies when necessary. I tell students in class, think about the little kid that wants something. They'll plead, beg, cry, barter, praise; always changing tactics. The best pivots happen when a person is checked into their audience and paying attention. We've all been in that situation where you can obviously see someone dropping interest or losing energy. Maybe it's a one on one situation with a coworker, friend or significant other. Maybe it's been in a meeting or a larger group. If you noticed the situation in the moment, did you change what you were doing or did you keep on your path, desperately hoping the audience would come back? Or, did you realize it after the fact and start kicking yourself for not taking action? It's a moment that can be improved with a conscious notice of the audience's attention and focus, and then a change in your strategy to get them back.

In improv, pivoting is necessary to move conversations along. You might come into a conversation with an idea and your partner speaks first before you get your idea out. It never fails, students come in with an idea and they can't get out of it, or move along with the idea that 'won' out. If I get in an improv conversation with you and call you 'Mom' before you define our relationship, even if you want to be a famous singer or sister or even dad – you are my mom. The reality of the situation has been established. There's much more on this idea in the section on 'Yes, And'. For now, it's important to note that once a conversation in improv gets started, whatever reality gets established is truth. Flexibility is key, you have to go with the moment – you also might have to pivot your preconceived notions regarding what's happening in the conversation.

Sounds a lot like adjusting our expectations for life, doesn't it? People tend to focus on their agenda far too often when speaking; they keep going even when their audience, whether it is one person or one hundred, is checked out. If you are paying attention to your audience and notice they are slipping, take a moment and reset. You can definitely go ahead and acknowledge that the audience is slipping – I've done this, and done everything from getting people up to stretch to having them turn and talk to their neighbor. The key is not to present this in a chiding 'you're not paying attention' way. This is much more effective with a 'hey I think I'm losing you, let's do something to get back together'. Sometimes transparency is the most authentic and effective solution! There are also a few vocal changes you can make to give you time to recalibrate and get your audience back. Learning to pivot will take time.

Our brains work in funny ways. Think about being around a constant and consistent noise. When I lived in NYC, traffic became akin to white noise. I didn't hear it after awhile and could very easily ignore it. Voices are similar! If your voice is moving at the same pace, volume and pitch, it can be blocked out if the listener loses attention. Thankfully we can change our voices. You can alter your cadence, which is the way your voice moves through space and you can throw in pregnant pauses. We all speak with personalized cadences, so any forced alteration will usually be different enough to jolt listeners back to the present moment. Adjusting this vocal quality can make your voice more dynamic and interesting. Back to the white noise of traffic – for those of you familiar, it's the difference between traffic and a siren. The change gets you to pay attention again.

First, let's visit the idea of pacing. We tend to speed up when we are excited about what we are talking about and slow down when we are trying to make an important point. This change comes fairly naturally – how often do you consciously think about changing your voice? The changes we do when we are excited or emphasizing a point cause a listener to tune in: why not develop these natural changes into a usable skill? Furthermore, when you speed up, your tone naturally rises and when you slow down, your tone lowers. A tonality change can also bring listeners back. These cadence alterations lead to a more dynamic style. The best speakers don't speak at the same speed or tone the entire time – they change things up. Monotone isn't going to cut it if you want your audience to pay attention.

Cadence alterations are just the beginning. Deliberate pauses are another powerful technique. Pregnant pauses are slightly longer than normal deliberate pauses, and all pauses can be used in many different ways. You can ask a question or make a statement that you'd like your audience to think about and then take a REAL silent pause. I'm not talking about a millisecond pause, one that's only discernible to you and your breathing. I'm talking about a real, pause, one where you count in your head for three seconds – one one-thousand, two one-thousand, three one-thousand – and then start speaking again. Be sure to give enough time to think about what you are asking them to do or time to answer your question.

Don't be afraid of the silence. Even if your audience isn't paying attention, that sudden controlled lack of noise snaps people out of whatever they were thinking about. Bring yourself back to high school, daydreaming about non-school things or doodling. You tuned back in, sometimes a few seconds too late, when the teacher asked you a question and there was a pause or a silence. Same idea! This trick brings people back without getting disciplined for not paying attention. Oh, and if they are listening? It gives them the time to process what they are hearing. Extra bonus: if you get comfortable in silence, you'll fix some of those filler words like 'um' and 'ah' that you might throw in when you don't know what to say next.

Try This

Find a friend or do this activity solo and practice cadence changes. Make a point to speed up, slow down, and purposely pause in a conversation or presentation. Make these changes exaggerated, which will make them unnatural. Don't worry, this isn't about you doing this all the time! You are just trying out tactics and ideas to see what fits with your personal style. Be sure to go from barely noticeable to over the top. An important thing to remember – this is ALL a change, so it might ALL feel a little strange. Incorporate some of the more comfortable cadence changes in every day conversation and public speaking to become a more dynamic speaker.

For this activity, if impromptu speaking is difficult, you can also try inserting these three alterations into text, regardless of what the text says, and then slowly start to incorporate them into every day impromptu conversation.

Pivoting and flexibility are not easy. You can control and increase your threshold and abilities through these activities and improv-based thinking. Keep in mind this growth won't happen all at once. You won't suddenly be chill and 'go with the flow' if flexibility triggers anxiety. Take each day and each success as it comes, and each failure as a learning experience. Focus on the growth.

Impromptu Speaking + Brain Locks

We are at the part of public speaking we can ALL identify with, no matter how you feel about speaking: a moment I like to call the brain lock. A brain lock can happen in a few different ways. You could go completely blank: everything leaves your head, all you can think about is the silence and the fact that everyone is staring right at you and oh no, they think you are unintelligent and a fool. Sound like a recent moment? Forced silences, ones that we <u>have</u> to take because we don't know what to say next, or because we lose track of our thoughts, aren't the same as pregnant pauses from our cadence activities. A pause is a controlled silence and a public speaking tool. A forced silence is akin to a brain meltdown. Another brain lock is a bit less of a work stoppage and brain strike and a bit more of a fixation. You suddenly can't think of anything except what you or someone else just said, or even something you were planning to say. Nothing else is coming and oh no, why can you only think about swimming, you don't even like to swim but it's what they just said and all you can think about is swimming! You keep running back and forth over the same thought and you can't get yourself out of the loop. Your brain is in a hamster wheel.

There's an activity I do with almost every single improv workshop that illuminates both of these points and helps shorten the recovery time between a brain lock and your ability to speak again. It's called 'What Are You Doing' and is easily one of my favorite activities for students – and me! – to see progress and growth. It starts with two people. Let's call them Person A and Person B. Person A starts doing any active activity and Person B asks, 'What are you doing?' Person A replies with anything but what they are actually doing, and Person B starts doing it. Person A then asks Person B, 'What are you doing?' and Person B replies with anything but what they are actually doing, and Person A starts doing it. It might look and sound something like:

Person A: (Dancing)
Person B: What are you doing?
Person A: Making a sandwich.
Person B: (Pretends to make a sandwich)
Person A: What are you doing?
Person B: Brushing my teeth.
Person A: (Pretends to brush teeth)

This goes back and forth, with people always saying one thing and doing another. Aside from focusing on brain locks and recovery time, this is also an activity in multi-tasking, that thing that is 'impossible' for our brains to do. There has been recent scholarship that suggests we can't actually multi-task. While I acknowledge the science behind the studies, the truth is we will still multi-task and will still be charged with doing multiple things at the same time. This activity dives right into the pressure of someone asking a pointed question and an audience watching you answer on the spot, or potentially struggle with a specific moment in time. It is a crash course in how we react during moments of brain locks.

Since this activity can be difficult and extremely helpful, I'm going to spend a little more time on the takeaways and pitfalls, as well as the scaffolding. 'What Are You Doing' is one of those activities that you could do every week for a month and you would see the most incredible improvement in a number of different areas of communication.

When I explain this activity in class, I get two students up to model the activity as I walk through it. This is a good time to repeat what I say in class: I'm intentionally and infuriatingly vague. Adults make a lot of rules that don't necessarily exist. We're quick to use the words 'can't' and 'shouldn't'. Who decides we can't? Often times we're just standing in our own way with these rules. We need to start thinking 'We can!' You <u>can</u> speak up, even if someone disagrees or thinks you aren't experienced enough to have an opinion. You <u>can</u> ask for a raise if you're expected to do more work. You <u>can</u> tell the guy next to you on the plane to get out of your personal space. You <u>can</u> make your own rules in life and your own path.

I also use this activity as a litmus test in class. I can immediately tell if someone is in their head, making rules or overthinking. Usually, the two students I have modeling the activity are nervously doing it correctly as I'm walking them through it and everyone else is nodding, either in semi-fear of their turn or with the opinion that this looks easy. Many of us watch people speak and judge how they did or judge how they are doing in any given moment, and think, 'I could do better.' We are human, it happens. This behavior feeds our fear of public speaking; we judge, so we know that others judge. Always remember it is easier to watch than to be on the spot.

The students that watch and are convinced they could do it better or faster or funnier than my models are genuinely surprised when it's their turn in front of the class. The moment they get up, all of their planning goes out the window. It's really quite easy to think of what you might say before it's your 'turn', it's a completely different thing to get up there, remember those things and pull it off. The same thing happens in meetings, dates, lives – that's where the 'ugh, I wish I said that' feelings comes from. Your brain sometimes just stops. It might fixate on something that's already been said. In this activity, your partner might say 'swimming'. Your fixation might be on all things swimming, and for some reason, all you can think about are ideas that involve swimming! You might also go completely blank. Your brain stops, and you can only think about the silence in the room, or the person asking 'what are you doing' or even the clock ticking. The activity ends in the same way every time for every person: you get done, sit down and think of a thousand things that you could have said. That feeling of 'I wish I thought of that sooner' is normal. People want to think faster and come up with witty and 'smart' responses. Repetition of the activity helps you think faster and respond with less of a lag. Because we are generally not asked to do these potentially silly things in real life, you're learning this skill set on a heightened plane.

The thing to remember with this activity, and most activities in this book, is the importance of scaffolding. Never start on a high level of difficulty because you might end up missing a very basic skill that can help you later in your journey. In this activity, you need to first be comfortable with the simple back and forth, saying one thing and doing another. After that, move into saying more than the three things you tried to plan before starting the activity. Once you master the back and forth, the next set of scaffolding includes using more than one word, adding vocalizations, and an elimination of the 'I ams'. The words 'I am' are filler; you're just giving yourself time to think of the next thing. The base version of this activity might sound like:

Person A: (Dancing)
Person B: What are you doing?
Person A: Swimming.
Person B: (Starts swimming in silence)

Person A: What are you doing?
Person B: Driving.
Person A: (Starts driving in silence)
Person B: What are you doing?
Person A: I…am…dancing.

The answers are one word, almost everything is done in silence, and the 'I am' is used to vamp for time. 'I am' in this activity is akin to a disfluency in speech. It's something that breaks up your normal speaking pattern. The fillers like 'um, ah, like' that we insert when we don't know what to say next? Those are disfluencies. We'll get more into disfluencies in the next section – for now, let's focus in on the scaffolded version of this activity. It might sound like:

Person A: (Dancing)
Person B: What are you doing?
Person A: Swimming a marathon.
Person B: (Starts swimming and saying 'splash, splash, splash')
Person A: What are you doing?
Person B: Driving with my mom.
Person A: (Starts driving and saying 'Mom, you're the worst back seat driver!')
Person B: What are you doing?
Person A: Dancing disco in the club.

The answers are more than one word, they are specific, they lack 'I ams' and there are vocalizations. These vocalizations can be dialogue or self narration, (Swim, Swim, Swim,) or a sound, like the sound effect of the water. This might feel silly, strange and a bit forced, especially the vocalizations. Here's the secret: this is super fun and immediately helpful. You know when you first discover something that is delicious AND healthy, like avocados? You are so pumped – this is good and good for me! This is the same thing. I've even had students tell me they taught and played this with friends at parties or at home with family because they love the results so much. In class, the difference between the easy version and the scaffolded version is immense. The easy version is silent and tense. We might be nervous for each other and we definitely are nervous about our upcoming or current turn. During the scaffolded version, people get laughs. I don't care what field you are in, or how shy or outgoing you might be, there is nothing better than making people laugh. It's a true form of joy to make someone laugh and if you make vocalizations and commit to your action, you WILL get laughs. When you do this, you find a level of comfort in vulnerability, and you let go. I assure newcomers that if they let go just a tiny bit, they too will laugh and feel free. We all take life and ourselves a bit too seriously. Personally, there is nothing better than seeing a student get their first or fiftieth laugh. It's usually greeted with an 'are they laughing AT me?' panic that's quickly replaced by an 'oh! I got this!' confidence.

The laughs come because people are committed and invested in the moment. When you are confident, you aren't telegraphing nervousness. Since no one is showing how nervous they are, the audience relaxes as well. Our audience gives us the energy we put out. If you're the focus and you walk into a room and are nervous, the audience feels uncomfortable. Same with excitement. If you're excited when you get up in front of an audience, they'll be excited for you. Furthermore, when you stop overthinking things, your brain stops locking. I had one student brainstorm things to say and do during this activity on the subway ride to class. She told me about this, and how unsuccessful it was because once it got to be her turn in class, she couldn't remember ANYTHING on the spot. When she let go and focused on the task, she let her thoughts stay in the moment. When she stayed in the moment, she realized that she stopped obsessing what the next 'right' answer was and got much faster in her response time. After she let go in class, she saw the same kind of interactions happen in every day life. Surprise! She was overthinking those too. When she was challenged with impromptu moments at work and in real life, she was able to come up with responses that conveyed what she actually wanted to say, because she stopped thinking about all of the possible responses and embraced the moment. It's a choice to stop overthinking things. It's a choice to be present.

When we overthink things, we sort through dozens of possibilities, stalling at ones that might be wrong and sometimes fixating on others. We also might focus on choices that are 'right' and worked in the past, and never try anything new. Impromptu speaking is difficult for so many people because of this 'right' and 'wrong' as well as the abundance of choices in the moment – or the appearance of choices. Too much creativity and freedom is just as crippling as not enough!

If you focus on the moment instead of being right or wrong in your answer, impromptu speaking is simple. It's all about being present, listening and responding. You are attending to the current moment, digesting it and reacting to it. Simple, right? The complicated part of impromptu speaking rests with the fear of making mistakes and the possibility of failure. What Are You Doing, while difficult, allows everyone to have some success and some room for improvement. Even in those moments when people think they 'failed' with this activity, they have actually succeeded, because they made it through and didn't have a complete meltdown. I think I've had two students in my history of teaching with EE that have told me they 'can't' do it, and only one of them actually just stopped and walked out of the room. She came back later, said she was having a terrible day and just couldn't think of anything else. The next time she did the activity? Nailed it because she gave in.

Try This

While you DEFINITELY can run this activity as described, acting it out and doing one thing while saying another, you can also do this with another person without the physical component. It's an 'exercise light' version for your body while still working your brain. The focus of What Are You Doing is directed at the ideas of being on the spot, multitasking and the other great skills described earlier; this non-physical version adds the scaffolded element of creativity while pushing further away from fixations on ideas. In this non-physical version, the base rules remain the same: you want to strive to respond with an activity that is in no way related to the current activity. When you are doing this activity in it's simplest form, you might not be aiming for creativity. It might sound like:

Person B: What are you doing?
Person A: Swimming in a pool. What are you doing?
Person B: Making a sand castle. What are you doing?
Person A: Throwing sand. What are you doing?

As you can see, answers might connect to the prior answer. It becomes more of an activity in general association and stream of consciousness than an activity in impromptu thinking, speaking and creativity. If you want to push your skills in those areas, the responses should not relate to the previous answer; they should be an organic 'stretch'. It might sound like:

Person B: What are you doing?
Person A: Swimming in a pool. What are you doing?
Person B: Eating nachos on the couch. What are you doing?
Person A: Thinking in the mountains. What are you doing?

You're forcing yourself to be creative and move away from the previous topic. Another way to make this even more impactful is to choose two letters to focus on. For example, you might choose 'S' and 'T'. Everything you are doing has to first start with an 'S' word and then a 'T' word sometime after that. It might sound like:

Person B: What are you doing?
Person A: Saving a taco. What are you doing?
Person B: Severing many tarantulas. What are you doing?
Person A: Soap taking. What are you doing?

Question: did you balk when I put the noun before the verb in that last example? Students will almost ALWAYS go 'verb noun' in this version of the activity, and I can't blame them! It's grammatically correct! The thing is, it's not a rule of the activity, just a rule in your head because it's proper grammar. The rules for this activity are saying one thing and doing another, no 'I ams', and using the two letters. The 'verb – noun' isn't a rule. You might argue and say, 'But we are making sentences!' We actually aren't – no 'I ams' remember? The scaffold of the letters and the focus on creativity are also adjustments that can be placed on the physical activity, if you choose. Both the physical and non-physical versions of the activity are important and helpful.

Some people tend to get stuck when the letters are initially put into use. A good tactic to get past that brain lock is to first breathe, then to start making the sounds of the letters versus thinking of the letters. For example, using that 'S' and 'T' from before, it's more effective to start making an 'S' sound instead of thinking 'S. What's an S word? Oh, it's quiet in here, why can't I think of an S word. S. S. S.' By making the sound, you give your brain time to relax, focus on that sound and escape the hamster wheel. People either love or hate the addition of the letters. It adds a parameter and 'rule' that helps focus in from too many options. Remember, too much creativity is sometimes just as bad as not enough. This is a great moment to check in with your own decisions and progress. Did you try What Are You Doing with all of the scaffolding elements? What version was easiest? Did you prefer more freedom or were you more creative with structure? I think a lot of creativity lies in being flexible within a structure – your structure just needs to be big enough to allow space for movement!

Try This

Find a friend and get ready to talk. Decide who is going to go first. That person is going to talk first. In this activity, you can talk about ANYTHING. If you need a prompt, here are a few ideas:

If you had 5 million dollars, what kind of business would you start and why?
If you could live anywhere, where would you live?
Where would you go on vacation if money wasn't an object?
If you could invent or create anything, what would you make?

Keep in mind with all of these prompts, failure is not an outcome – everything you want is yours and you will be successful. The person who isn't talking is listening, and also saying one of two things: 'Zoom In' or 'Zoom Out'. They can say these prompts at any time, and the speaker has to follow the direction associated with the phrase. Zoom In prompts the speaker to get more detailed about the last thing that they said. Zoom Out is the opposite, the speaker should get less detailed. It might sound something like:

Person A: This weekend I was thinking about getting some groceries, maybe bake a tart, watch some movies…
Person B: Zoom In on movies.
Person A: I was thinking about scary movies because scary movies are the best if it's a rainy weekend. If I watch a scary movie too late I have to sleep with the lights on.
Person B: Zoom Out.
Person A: After those movies, I might make pasta and then clean the house…

This activity will help you exist in the moment, and focus on flexibility in impromptu speaking, especially if your partner calling Zoom In and Zoom Out is calling the prompts when they want to learn more or less. It's not helpful for them to stay silent (what do you learn?) or for them to be a jerk and call the prompts constantly to the point the person can't catch up. They should be called when your partner wants to know more details or get the bigger picture.

Aside from being flexible to the whim of a partner's interest, Zoom In, Zoom Out shows the speaker what an audience might be interested in. If your partner is calling In or Out when they want to know more or are over the minutia of a topic, we can learn what areas are of interest to others and what areas simply interest us. At times, we can be way more interested than our audience in a subject or we completely underestimate the interest of our audience! I can't tell you how many times students tell me 'I was worried I was boring my partner'. The moment you start worrying is the moment your audience feels worry for you. Figuring out an audience takes attention and practice, and this activity is a great entry point in developing the skill to read an audience.

Impromptu speaking sounds much scarier than it actually is. Getting through that fear starts by working on flexibility and paying attention to the moment. If you are listening carefully and practice responding to the moment right in front of you, it's less about being intimidated by something that sounds as big as 'impromptu speaking' and more about just having a dialogue.

The 'It Factor' + Presence

We've all seen *that* speaker. You know the one; you can't take your eyes off of her. She could be talking about ANYTHING and you would hang on her every word. I'm not talking about the idea of heroes and super fans – we all know that *other* person that we'd do anything to see. One of my Sheroes, Barbara Corcoran, could read the phone book and I'd be cheering for those numbers. It's not that. This is all about presence and the 'It Factor', which is that something extra that really makes a speaker special. I've debated this, argued about this and disagreed with so many coaches about what this is. I still firmly believe it all comes down to one thing: confidence.

Think about the last time you spoke in front of other people. How did you feel about it? Were you confident or nervous? Did you feel awkward or passionate? Whatever you felt, your audience felt it too. I say this, and have intentionally said this so many times already, because we often forget it. The energy you put out is the energy the audience feels and reflects back. It ping pongs back and forth and amplifies.

If you walk into a room and your first thought is 'ugh, I don't want to be here' the audience will feel like they don't want to be there. If you walk in and your first thought is 'wow, I'm so excited to be here!' the audience will also feel excited to be there.

You get what you give.

Since speaking is a personal interaction between you and the audience, with you talking to them instead of at them, you have to care about what you're saying and show it. If you don't care, why should they? If you feel awkward or nervous the whole time, and afterward reflect that the audience seemed tense, you might be doing yourself a disservice if you blame your topic. Your energy is coming back at you, because <u>how</u> you say things is just as important as what you say.

Practice in improv is practice in confidence. Think about it, would you willingly get up in front of a room full of coworkers or strangers and be 100% silly? Probably not. If you have to get up there, wherever and whatever there is, and it's apparent that you feel awkward, everyone is going to feel terribly awkward FOR you. On the other hand, want to or not, if you go out there and you own it, you will look confident and people won't be able to take their eyes off of you.

So how do you grow confidence? There are plenty of resources and books out there on gaining self-confidence and working on how you feel about yourself, quieting that inner critic and stopping imposter syndrome. The foundation of improv is based around an idea that exudes confidence: fake it. In improv, you're the best at whatever you're doing. Even if you don't know how to do something, you fake it, and you do it to the best of your ability. I tell students, especially in What Are You Doing, do it, whatever it is, like you are being paid millions of dollars. Add motivation! The scaffolded version of What Are You Doing is a great example of this. Say you're practicing with letters and someone tells you to sever a tarantula.

Ok right now, visualize what that looks like. Whatever you think of is right.

And...

GO! Do it! Sever away!

I have NO idea what severing a tarantula looks like. Does it involve chopping off legs? Is it sword-fighting? Do you pretend to cut a spider in half? No clue. And it <u>does not matter.</u> What matters is the idea of owning that severing when the situation calls for it. If you get up there and sever tarantulas with dedication and gusto, you'll look amazing and everyone will watch you and laugh, not because you look ridiculous, but because you are committing. If you get up and say 'I don't know what that is' or awkwardly stand there, everyone watching will feel awkward for you. That confidence makes the difference between an awkward moment and an incredible moment.

Another activity that builds confidence revolves around you being an expert about something – the last few I've had in class have been bugs, film, the circus and children. Someone else chooses your expertise – knowing you probably aren't an expert in that field – and then starts asking you questions, which you will answer 'correctly' *no matter what*. Sure, if you gave the same answers on a test in school, you'd get it wrong. In this particular activity, whatever you say is correct. One of the best examples came from a continuing education class. The speaker was a bug expert and another student asked why bugs don't get as big as people. The 'Bug Expert' went on and on about how they used to be that big and aren't anymore because of the fluoride in the water, selling his answer to us. While we knew we were doing an activity to focus on 'selling it' and believing in an answer, I couldn't help but believe our Bug Expert just a little. It was that convincing. On the flip side, if you worry in this exercise about being 'right' regarding something that has no consequence, no attachment to your actual job, and potentially something you know nothing about, you might have a hard time showing confidence in things you actually DO know a lot about.

Translate both of those activities to public speaking. If you own what you're saying and commit, avoiding disfluencies, standing or sitting strong and talking to an audience, not to your paper or notes or computer, you'll look more confident than nervous. Even if you are shaking inside, you'll start to feel confident if you start committing fully to what you're doing. Think about how you feel doing something you absolutely love to do. Whatever that is, whether it be cooking, dancing, or traveling – think about it and connect with that feeling. You probably don't get nervous doing something you love with all your being, right? Think about that right before you start speaking. Those good feelings and that confidence will bleed into your speaking. The passion you have for what you love doing? That passion makes the audience feel great and makes you fascinating. The 'It Factor' isn't just about loving what you are doing; you have to show that you feel great doing it.

Another way to show that you are enjoying yourself? Smile.

Before I get into the why behind smiling, there's an activity I do with students to loosen them up in the beginning of class that centers on emotions and emotional states. The students start walking around a room in 'neutral'. They are walking like they do on a normal day in a normal manner. Then, they start to embody different emotions as I call them. This isn't just a facial embodiment; it's a full body expression. If I call the emotion of 'happy', the group will show happiness at its most extreme. Take a moment to check in and think about what happiness looks like on your body and in how you move. For me, I smile and move faster than my normal pace. The next emotion for the group might be 'nervous' and they embody nervousness at 100% intensity. What does that look like on you? I tend to tense my shoulders and cross my arms with an awkward smile. Would you rather telegraph how you look when you are happy or how you look when you are nervous?

Now, back to the smile advice. I've gotten a lot of flak on this due to the stereotype of people telling women to smile because they 'look prettier when they smile.' This tip applies to men and women, and it isn't about smiling to look more attractive. It *is* all about what we do when we are happy, confident and friendly – we smile. It will relax you and ease any nerves that are creeping in. You will LOOK confident and that's what 'fake it till you make it' is all about. Looking like something before you feel it, until you feel it. Extra win with the smile? Your cadence changes! Your voice is noticeably brighter when you smile – go ahead and try. Say something with a huge smile and then say something with an expression of apathy. Feel the difference?

Finally, how do you feel about what you are saying? Does it sound like you, and do you believe in it? If you aren't being authentic, it's not going to be something people want to listen to. I was working an event a few years ago and the keynote speaker was this huge deal in the sales and marketing world. Everyone was excited to hear him speak. Yet I had no fewer than four people come up to me and ask why they couldn't pay attention while he was speaking. My answer? They had an idea of who this person was, read his books and his social media, and the person that was actually speaking onstage wasn't who they expected. He sounded like he was yelling at the audience while talking about connecting to customers, and was awkwardly using the audience member's names in his keynote. It wasn't a 'let me ask you a real question after noticing your name badge' thing; it was a 'let me glance at your name badge and use the same person in every single example for the next five minutes'. It was awkward and incredibly ineffective because this guy was completely disingenuous.

Unlike this keynote speaker who was widely published and had a large social media presence and voice, we usually aren't typed before we walk in the door. That being said, you have to maintain a style that is authentic to you, otherwise, it will look and sound unnatural. You also have to understand how you feel, and that will be discussed in further detail with self-awareness in the last section of this book. One thing to always remember: be the best version of yourself. It doesn't matter how your friend speaks, how your boss moves her head, how your sister-in-law stands – what matters is what feels right for YOU in the situation that you're in, speaking directly to that unique audience. These tips and lessons can offer polish for improvement, and they also help develop and bring out the best version of YOU.

Last quick confidence fix? Sit or stand strong. If you start crossing your legs and arms tightly, spinning rings on your hands, taking up too little or too much space with your body, you're going to look nervous. Place your feet as solidly as possible on the floor and release any tension you might be holding. If you don't know if you are holding tension, quickly tense up areas of your body starting at your feet and holding the tension for three seconds, letting it out on an exhale.

Confidence and presence could be a book in and of itself. Unfortunately, with some people – myself included – it can change on a semi-daily and daily basis. We're all works in progress, constantly striving to be better. Until we get to a point we feel satisfied with the level of confidence we have, we might just have to pretend until it's real. At a seminar I learned that if you put a pencil or pen between your teeth and hold it, you activate the same muscles as smiling, and you start to feel happier. True or not, it's worked every single time for me. If I'm feeling low and heading in to teach or a meeting, I put a pen between my teeth. This is the same idea as fake it till you make it. No one knows you're faking it except **you**.

Being on the Spot: Deal with It

A few years ago, I had a student that was really upset in class with being on the spot. It was midway through a three-week series, and the class had a few new people as well as a few returning students. We finished the opening warm up and were moving on to longer improvised conversations. During our first reflection of the night, she said she felt uncomfortable in class. When I asked why, she said she didn't appreciate being put on the spot. I asked other students in the class how they felt, and the class agreed with the idea of discomfort in being on the spot, and as one student put it, 'At least we are all equally ridiculous.' When pushed further, they discovered something I already knew – that people don't often go out of their way to be on the spot. We avoid it in real life, unless we live for the spotlight.

I avoid hip-hop dancing too. I took one class and felt awful.

Guess what? I'm still awful at hip-hop even though I am a dancer. I avoid it, so I never give myself a chance to get better. Sure, maybe my body doesn't move like that. I don't know. I didn't like how I felt, so I never went back.

The same happens with people on the spot. Avoidance does not lead to improvement. Not by a long shot.

In the earlier example, even though the other students didn't like being on the spot, they didn't avoid it in class. The student that voiced her dislike and discomfort? She avoided it in class. She would deflect decisions to her partners, make half-statements and shirk away from any initiative that might put her on the spot. Her opinion was just as valid as the other students. She hated being on the spot. Guess what? She isn't alone.

Why do we dislike being on the spot in the first place? Along with the earlier thoughts on brain locks and impromptu speaking, we tend to remember the terrible experiences more than the great ones. Sometimes it's residual stress and anxiety, and sometimes it's a feeling of failure from past moments when things haven't gone quite right. That stress and anxiety around failure isn't a good feeling. Unfortunately, we can't change our memories, we can just rework how we feel about things by having new adventures. With improv, you're supposed to be out in the open, vulnerable and somewhat exposed. You're meant to be on the spot. And sometimes? You feel like you fail. If you fail in improv, much like in the real world, life moves on, and you gain a comfort level with unexpected outcomes.

If you never get comfortable being on the spot, you'll never become a better public speaker. Public speaking is all about being on the spot! The attention is on you, and there is no way to plan it all. There are two stories I want to share with you about being on the spot. One went viral and the other is unique to EE.

Viral first: In 2014, Michael Bay was speaking at the Consumer Electronic Show. He was talking with Joe Stinziano, Samsung's Vice President, about a Samsung television product and his teleprompter went out. Out as in, he couldn't read the words on the screen. Bay started visibly panicking. Stinziano tried to improvise with Bay, asking him questions about his movies and the product. Bay froze. Cringe-worthy semi-silent moments went by, and finally Bay got so flustered he walked off stage. The internet, as usual, went nuts with criticism. Bay issued a statement afterward saying that he wasn't 'great' with live shows. His on the spot moment where things went differently than expected? Crash and burn. He got so nervous and stuck in his head that he couldn't even answer simple questions or focus on the moment in front of him.

EE moment: In 2014, I was teaching a group of students in NYC. There happened to be a lot of single people in class, and quite a few of them scheduled dates after class. You might ask why would ANYONE go on a date <u>after</u> improv class. One woman put it perfectly: this class was practice for any and all crazy date situations. She was a special needs coordinator for a large organization, had quite a few years of experience with pretty stressful situations, and in my opinion, was pretty collected through all of them. She shared that she got incredibly nervous being asked questions on a first date, and since practicing improv, she stopped being so nervous. I asked what, specifically, about the class prepped her for dates, and she said, 'In an hour and a half, I managed to throw myself on the floor in front of a car and practiced saying and doing crazy and unrealistic things starting with 'M' and 'K'. The questions on my date? Nothing compares to what I do in class.' Those on the spot moments of silliness and ridiculousness from class made everything else in life that much easier.

Would world-renowned director Michael Bay have been better in his Samsung moment if he had practiced being on the spot? Uncertain. Can practicing and getting to know yourself when you are on the spot help you when you're actually on the spot? You bet. The lack of control in those moments builds on our fear of the unknown. While the unknown is scary, you can work on increasing your comfort level being on the spot. You *could* just put yourself on the spot more often and throw yourself into situations, unprepared and flying by the seat of your pants. Doesn't sound like the best of ideas, especially if you're already nervous. Aside from taking an improv class, there are a few ways to work those skills. You CAN start to reflect on how you feel while you are on the spot. Think of the last time you were on the spot. Ask yourself the following questions:

What kind of situation was it?
How did you feel before?
How did you feel after?
How did it go?
How could it have gone better?
How could you have prepped better?

These questions reveal A LOT about how you feel being on the spot. Was it a situation that you could have prepped for or was it truly impromptu? Were you having a good day or a bad day before the situation? Even the best speakers can get sidetracked by a terrible day. Afterward, were you relieved, exhausted, tired? It could have gone great and you might just be overthinking it.

Now, how could it have gone better? Did you speak to your audience? Did you talk at them? Did you have things you wish you had said?

And finally, how could you prep better? Is this a situation that happens often or is it something completely new? Is it a meeting that happens every week or something like an interview question or first date moment that threw you off guard?

After you've reflected on the situation, it's time to think about the next one. Work on the things you can and do the preparation that you could have done. As for the things that were out of your hands? Let them go. If they are things that you truly have no control over – let them go and prepare for the things you can, and control the aspects that are controllable.

Being on the spot becomes easier the more you attend to the moment in front of you. Those times when we are asked to do something mortifying on the spot? I think those are the things of nightmares. In the real world, I don't think we're really ever asked to do something embarrassing in front of a group of strangers. Those dreams of singing, dancing and naked public speaking in front of every person on the planet? They are stress nightmares and are not real. I do have an activity that you CAN do with a group, if you want to practice those moments of potential mortification around people you love – or like enough to be vulnerable with. Hot Spot is a fun yet sometimes terrifying activity for groups. You stand in a circle with one person in the center. That person starts singing a song (SEE, <u>this</u> is why it's not listed as a Try This activity!) When the group knows the song they are singing, they sing along. At any point during the song, someone can walk to the person in the center, tap them on the shoulder, take their place in the center and start singing a new song that the group will hopefully sing along to. The song doesn't have to connect to the current song, or any future song. Whatever comes to your head is correct.

Aside from being slightly terrifying to sing in front of people you know or don't know, in public, not in the shower or car, this activity is all about getting up there in the 'spotlight' and owning it. If you are singing enough for the group to recognize the tune, they will sing along because they also don't want to be stuck in the center, alone, singing by themselves. They help you, you help them. Something to keep in mind on the outside of the circle: you don't want the person in the center to die. You want to back them up, vocally or humming or dancing – you also want to jump up there and take your turn as soon as you can so they don't fall apart in the center. No one has to see the song connection except for you – it's complete stream of consciousness, which means you can totally plan what you're going to sing. You just have to get up there and do it.

I LOVE doing this activity with groups, and I know quite a few workplaces that still do this activity before big meetings or conferences. It not only gets everyone jazzed up – the tension and release of singing in public is pretty amazing – it also gets everyone looking out for one another. Don't you want that when you're about to be on the spot? To know that other people have been there too, that other people have felt like the world was going to swallow them up and they are still here to talk about it? When I do teach this activity to groups, if the group is on the smaller side (under 20 people) everyone has to go in order for the activity to end. Everyone has to experience the vulnerability.

I'm not a sadist. I do think that we don't have many opportunities to 'try' being on the spot, until it's a real moment ON THE SPOT. Think about Hot Spot – if you sing in front of people and you live through it (which you will) how easy will the rest of the day/week/month be?

Before closing this section on public speaking, I have to bring up a common argument from students in class. Often times, I'll have one student per class that will argue with me on the importance of how we say things versus what we say. 'My words matter more than how I stand/speak/pause/use filler words.' And it never fails, we'll get into the idea of people just being themselves, and how it's important to be yourself and authentic. Yes, you have to be yourself, unapologetically so. You also have to speak <u>to</u> the audience in front of you and adjust to the situation you are in. If you're going into a new/stressful/important/ professional situation, why wouldn't you want to be incredibly prepared and have all of the chips stacked in your favor? Take care of the known quantities and prep – that way, those unknown things that come up are far less scary. I'm constantly telling students, there is no one 'right' way with public speaking; it's about talking TO your audience and being the best version of yourself. How you say things does matter – you wouldn't speak to a kindergartener the same way you'd talk to a coworker, right? You should adjust yourself to your specific audience. You're still you; you are just bringing out the version of yourself best suited for that particular audience and situation. That flexibility and ability to read an audience comes with time and practice. The ability to read an audience is simply about paying attention, listening, and developing focus.

Improv and public speaking go hand in hand. While a lot of the activities in this section are about warming up and preparing for speaking, it's based on the idea of going to the gym for your brain. You can't sit back and do nothing and expect to get better at something. You don't sit back and expect to be magically fluent in another language or wake up a piano prodigy. Why expect to suddenly get better at public speaking? Great public speakers aren't born, they are made. If you truly want to become a better public speaker, practice flexibility, pivoting, confidence, impromptu speaking and being on the spot. Focus on your energy when you walk into a room, and make sure to check in with any anxiety that you have. That anxiety can and will bleed into your audience – and so will your confidence, even if you're faking it. Impromptu speaking is much easier if you are listening and focusing on the moment at hand. Listening is a choice, just like putting yourself on the spot. You can choose to prepare, choose to focus, choose to listen, and choose to embrace the moment in front of you, or you can choose to ignore and avoid it and continue to think that you just aren't good at it.

Finding Your Communication Style

According to the National Association of College and Employers 2016 Job Outlook report, verbal communication skills are the most important skill sought in new candidates. On a 5-point scale, verbal communication skills were rated 4.63, coming in ahead of teamwork (4.62) and the ability to make decisions and solve problems (4.49).

While this data is unsurprising, it makes a stronger case for building communication skills. Even for those who are already employed and not job seeking, some of the largest problems at work occur when communication fails. How often have you wished you could redo a meeting, or been proactive and forward thinking enough to ask for more information in the moment when something wasn't quite clear? Maybe you misheard or misunderstood a coworker, and that resulted in a problem. Or maybe you haven't been listening as well as you should, and you fixated on what you 'have' to get done that you miss an incredible opportunity? Your professional communication skills might need work.

Now consider the last problem you had with a friend, family member or significant other. Think about it, as much as possible, without emotion, and break it down to its base issue. Was it a communication breakdown or misunderstanding that was at the root of the problem? Your personal communication skills might need work.

I remember in undergrad, I saw the major of 'Communications' and was curious about what they could possibly teach that people didn't already naturally do. As an adult that has had her fair share of distracted moments, misunderstandings on professional and personal levels as well as confusing-just-because-I-didn't-listen-well-enough moments, I think back to that cavalier attitude about communication that I had in undergrad. Now that I'm in the practice of teaching communication skills, I have an understanding of some nuanced information. Practice in improv is practice in communication by having conversations. There are a few key differences:

- There is an audience of your fellow classmates and a teacher
- This audience can eavesdrop without looking weird or creepy
- You get a redo after your 'woulda, coulda, shoulda'
- Your teacher can and should coach and reflect with you

The woulda, coulda, shoulda is that terrible feeling you might experience after conversations or interactions. If I only had thought more I would have said this, if I only had more time I could have said that, if I only knew I should have said this. While we don't usually get a redo of a conversation in life, in improv, every moment is a new moment, and you can always try for that redo without a single consequence.

Imagine two people having a conversation. One person says something, and the other person responds to what that person says, and the first person responds to that response. These people don't know what the other is going to say and are reacting and responding to that moment. They have to listen to the other person, because if they don't, they miss something in the situation. That's verbal communication.

That's improv.

Listening

We can be terrible listeners. There is no way around it; every person on the planet could dedicate time to becoming a **better** listener. We don't listen as well as we should because our attention is often divided. Right now, check in. Are you thinking about other things happening today, tomorrow, next week? I'm not offended – we're busy! We have things going on! We have to divide our time, multi-task, think about what's happening tomorrow, next week, what happened yesterday, what we are making for dinner, what work we have to get done – how can we be expected to fully listen and pay attention to what's happening in front of us?

Generally speaking, unless we have bad hearing or are always at a rock concert, we can hear each other just fine. *Listening* and *hearing* are two different things. Hearing happens naturally; it's simply the act of perceiving sound. Listening, on the other hand, is a conscious choice. We have to choose to tune in and pay attention. Often times we choose to half listen because we are thinking about a dozen things that may or may not connect to the conversation we are currently taking part in.

If two people are having a conversation in improv class, they have to listen to **every single thing**. One of the most basic activities in class is the three-line conversation. Within three lines of dialogue, two individuals need to establish 'who' they are, specifically 'what' their relationship is to one another, and 'where' they are. A line of dialogue could be a single word or it could be a five-minute rant. It's more about a person making a statement, someone responding to that statement, and that first person responding to that response. When you practice an improv conversation, you can be anyone and anywhere you want to be, and you do not discuss it with your partner ahead of time. You could choose to be yourself, or you could choose to be the mayor of New York. You could choose to be inside your house, or on the interstate in Hawaii. The sky is truly the limit in the creation of a who and a where within improv conversations. Connecting to this, one of the larger rules of improv is the idea of saying 'Yes'. The principle of 'Yes, And' will be explained shortly, and for now, we'll focus on the Yes. If someone claims to be the mayor of New York, that person is the mayor of New York. If you wanted them to be your mom, that person *can* be your mom. That person is also the mayor of New York. You have to always say Yes to the reality of the situation. For example, the three-line conversation could sound like:

Person A: Mom, can I borrow the car?
Person B: Only if you do these dishes first. The kitchen is a mess.
Person A: Ugh, fine, I'm only washing these. Someone else can clean the stove.

It's important to note that Person B didn't say, 'Yes, take the car!' Free choice still exists in improv. They did take on the role of 'mom' without question. Through this conversation, we know they are mother and child, and the conversation is taking place in the kitchen. The 'who' and 'where' are clear. The heightened and by result active listening comes from creating that reality. Both individuals need to carefully listen to determine what had been established and what needs more information or clarification. That state of heightened listening is necessary in improv conversations in order to establish a reality. Without that, it's just two people talking at one another. As the improv conversations get longer than three lines, this skill is even more important. Through a longer conversation, more of the reality of the situation is uncovered, and through this, more information is given from and to each person. With more information, the possibility of errors increases, as you have more to listen, remember and pay attention to.

The 'wrong' in a three-line conversation would be a person not listening and not accomplishing the task of establishing who and where. It might sound like:

Person A: Hi, how are you?
Person B: Whew it's hot here in the desert. I'm fine mom, how are you?
Person A: Well I'm good sonny, come into the kitchen and give your grandpa a kiss.

Person A clearly didn't listen to the 'mom' or 'desert' choices and created their own who and where instead of playing off what the other person said. While this is a slightly extreme example, it's happened. You get so caught up in the activity and outcome that you forget to focus on the main point of the activity: listening. Think about life now: how often have you gotten into a conversation with someone, knew what you had to talk about and either never got around to it or never hit the point because of a listening mishap? Same idea. When you listen, you have to make the choice to actively pay attention and focus on the moment.

I witnessed one of the most extreme examples of poor listening skills when I was leading a group of engineers in longer conversations as part of their training on, you guessed it, listening skills. A man and a woman got up and started their conversation. The woman started dancing and immediately said, 'Dad, do you think I'm good enough to be on American Bandstand?' The man replied, 'Yeah, yeah,' and went back to pretending to read a newspaper. The conversation progressed, and the woman kept dancing and the man kept reading his paper. Every once in awhile, he put it down to look up while they talked about mundane things. It felt awkward. Anytime you are eavesdropping on a conversation, which is what improv practice is, you feel a little awkward.

I shouldn't have been feeling awkward though! At this point, I had been teaching for awhile and A LOT, so I've seen the strangest of dynamics and eavesdropped on loads of improv conversations. There must be something in the relationship, I thought...

Wait...

The more I watched, the more I realized exactly what was happening in front of us, and THAT was the awkwardness, not the voyeurism of the situation. Something just wasn't right with this father and daughter dynamic, and I was becoming surer and surer by the second what it was. Finally, after a few moments, the man interrupted the woman mid-sentence and said, 'This is the weirdest strip club I've ever been to!'

The room got deathly quiet.

I was right.

I bookended the conversation with, 'And give them a round of applause!' (Side note, we don't applaud enough for one another. It feels awesome. Let's do it more, as much as possible. Try it sometime, it's amazing.) Per usual, I asked the group to reflect on what just happened. Kicking off the conversation, I looked at the man and said, 'That was an interesting choice, what made you make it?' knowing full well what happened. 'Well you told me any choice was a good one,' he said, almost defiantly, clearly thinking I was upset about his strip club reference. 'Sure,' I replied, 'and she's your daughter, so it was a bit of a *different* choice.' He immediately replied with, 'No she isn't,' to which everyone in the room, including the director of HR, said and nodded in agreement with me. The woman in the conversation with him looked at him and just said, 'Yep.'

To this day, I have never seen a man that mortified.

He simply wasn't listening. The entire company, CEO, HR, their Houston branch – everyone was there. They flew people to NYC for this training. This wasn't 'guy humor'. This was someone who was not used to actively listening. He might have heard what she said in the beginning about dancing. He missed the 'dad' from her very first sentence. And who knows what he missed in everyday conversations, both at work and in his personal life, all because he didn't actively listen. He had no idea what a terrible listener he WAS, and actually thanked me after class for nudging (kicking) him to think more about his listening skills.

As nice of a teaching/learning/validation moment this was, he's not the first or the last person to suffer from terrible listening skills. He's also one of the very few lucky ones to have it called out, in real time, so he can hopefully learn from the mistake. We aren't so lucky in every day life – we usually have these moments and don't realize we're having them until it's too late! Lucky for everyone, heightened listening can be learned – I tell students to always listen like everyone is watching.

Try This

The next time you have a conversation with someone, focus on what they are saying and listen. Let that other person talk at length about whatever they want to talk about. Maybe you are sitting and listening to a friend or spouse talk about their day, or a coworker talk about a new idea. Be silent and let them talk. While they are talking, listen for these two things:

1. Identify what they are talking about. Pick out two points and silently note them. Maybe it's the point of the conversation, the problem they are discussing, or the event from the day. Whatever it is, consciously identify two points.

2. Think of a specific question that you could ask to get more information. It could be to clarify what they are saying to get deeper in the issue or to find out more details about some item you find interesting. Find a moment (not right away!) to ask that question. Be careful with questions that insert <u>you</u> into the conversation. We all have that person in our lives that always has a 'me too' to add. Shared moments are lovely; a person that inserts a 'me too' simply to turn the conversation back to them is selfish. Know <u>why</u> you ask the question and be sure to use a question to connect, not to hijack the conversation.

With listening, you need to not only listen; you need to also <u>show</u> you listen. Just nodding and smiling isn't enough. The people that nod and smile a lot are extremely giving individuals. They could also be thinking about other things and doing what they think they should be doing to show they are listening. They might be thinking about dinner, a date, what they are doing later and what they think they should be working on. By using the above exercise naturally in conversation – not talking, discovering the point, identifying and asking a specific question – you are engaged in the conversation and actively listening.

This is not to say that non-verbal communication is moot when it comes to listening! If you are a person that nods and smiles when someone is talking, please don't stop. When people are nervous about talking to a large group, I tell them to look for you – I look for you in a large group! Be sure you are doing it because you agree, are excited, want to be supportive – and are listening. Please don't just do it because it makes you look present.

Listening is the base of all communication. Without this crucial skill, all conversations in improv and in life will fall apart into missed points and misunderstandings. The idea of ACTIVE listening can be a lot more daunting than simply attending to the person in front of you. While it's a relatively simple idea once you turn your brain 'on', it often gets pushed to the side when we get to the reasons for our conversations. Everyone has an agenda.

Agenda-Orientated Thinking

In improv, you are almost always working on multiple things at the same time. Two major ones: making the person you're working with look good and moving the conversation forward. Improv isn't a solo opportunity to shine and you aren't trying to 'win' anything. This is why so many teambuilding activities are based in improv pedagogy – improv is a team sport. Which is yet another reason it lends itself to improving communication skills: a conversation needs more than one person.

Miscommunications don't just happen because of poor listening. They also happen because of agenda-orientated thinking, which can cause you to miss information by fixating on what you 'need' to say, instead of listening to the person in front of you. How often have you considered the lens with which you view information and situations? Distracted and half-listening can occur because we are thinking about our own personal agenda. This leads to agenda-orientated thinking, which is also responsible for that pesky auto responder that turns on in our brain. It's that feeling when we think we need to say what we <u>need</u> to say, regardless of what gets said to us. Think of the last time you got on a plane or went to a movie. Did the person checking your ticket say, 'Have a nice flight' or 'Enjoy the show'? Probably. Did you reply, 'You too!'

That person isn't flying or seeing a movie.

Those automatic responses are one type of agenda-orientated thinking. This type centers on the idea that someone says something to you and you want to, or think you have to, return the favor by saying something back. You aren't listening to pay attention; your focus is just beyond the point of hearing because you are responding in the most basic definition of responding. You aren't moving the conversation forward naturally or offering additional information. The same thing happens when someone says, 'How are you today?' and you reply, 'Fine, how are you?' and they say, 'Fine, how are you?' That double-ask is an automatic response. If you're sitting here overthinking the times you may or may not have been that person, don't beat yourself up. It happens to all of us. That auto responder comes into play when we are distracted, tired or focused on other things. I did it recently, and realized it in the moment. I laughed, acknowledged that it happened, and immediately adjusted to focus. Once you know it happens, the adjustment is easy. Pay attention to interactions and listen to what other people are saying to you and what you are saying to them. It's thinking about the moment and focusing on what's happening around you in the present moment, because focus is just as important as listening. You can't just float in and out of conversations; just like listening and hearing, you have to make a choice to pay attention and not let your mind wander. If you have an automatic response and realize it in the moment? Have a laugh with the other person. Transparency is powerful. Call yourself out and move forward, choosing to be present. You can also silently acknowledge it and choose to pay attention to the current moment. It's all a choice.

The other kind of agenda-orientated thinking isn't as easy to solve. This kind involves a focus on intent versus the give and take of communication. There's an innate desire to say whatever you need to say, regardless of what the other person says. It's very one-sided. Since improv and life aren't about one person, they don't work without a give and take relationship. One person can't focus everything in a conversation on himself or herself; we have to listen to one another. One of the greatest examples of this kind of agenda-oriented thinking I've ever witnessed happened in a public class. We were doing three-line conversations and the situation went something like this:

Person A: Ok, when you get inside, just go up to the counter and get the money. Don't talk to anyone else; just get the money and go.
Person B: Right, we got this. You keep the car running and I'll be out as soon as possible. I won't shoot anyone.
Person A: Shoot anyone!? This is your first time withdrawing money at the bank, you're 15!

The participants and the other students looked confused. Me too.

Our reflection opened with a 'so how do you feel?' and was greeted with expressions of 'um, what just happened?' by the whole group. Turns out, Person A, a museum professional, was so set on his idea of taking his daughter to the bank and having an awkward 'first bank trip' that he couldn't move from his agenda when Person B, a career counselor, made it about a robbery. Everyone in the room saw it as a robbery and they were completely lost with this idea that came out during reflection of 'baby's first bank trip.'

As mentioned earlier, the flexibility to move and pivot within the moment is something that's developed through awareness, reflection and practice. If you are present in the moment and your conversation takes a sharp turn, and you are actively listening, you can easily turn with it because all you are doing is that first step of listening: responding to the moment. This also means you have to learn to drop your original planned agenda if it isn't working out. The problem in the above situation was that Person A didn't make his idea completely clear, so Person B made a choice to complete the objective of the activity, and Person A, instead of going along with her new idea to finish, kept pushing his idea. He didn't just exhibit agenda-orientated thinking; he also showed how inflexible he was in that moment, which is often a trait of agenda-oriented thinkers. They are centered on their immediate goals and often can't see the bigger picture and objective. They also might lack the ability to be flexible in the moment and change their original plan. At some point or another, we all exhibit agenda-orientated thinking. Just like poor listening, it's a choice to improve this skill.

There's generally a lot of confusion surrounding agenda-oriented thinking versus trying to get what you want, so let me make this very clear: They are not the same thing. Agenda-orientated thinking is a fixation on a goal with little to no regard to the current situation. We've all talked to those people who are so focused on what they want that you either need to give in or give up. Trying to get what you want is also a skill enhanced with improv, and it's focused on listening to your audience, whoever that may be, and working with them to accomplish something, not steam-rolling them to an end goal. Agenda-oriented thinking in conversation is the idea of saying 'that's great, so I've been wanting to ask you something…' even if your friend just told you that she's having the worst day. Working on what you want is noting her bad day, offering some chocolate and then asking her the favor after you've let her cry it out, or waiting for a better time. It's attending to the situation first, then getting to what you want and need, while acknowledging the reality in the moment. It goes back again to being in the present and responding to the situation.

Wants are a bit more nuanced than simple agenda-orientated thinking. I often compare the latter to Einstein's idea that 'insanity is doing the same thing over and over and expecting a different result'. Agenda-orientated thinkers usually don't take into account other aspects of the situation. They usually continue to push and push regardless if it's working or not. On the flip side, think of the little kid in the grocery store who wants candy. That little kid will cry, beg, plead, bargain. They will change tactics when one isn't working. Getting what you want as an adult should be very similar – it's all about the pivot. Within improv, wants are crucial. If the individuals conversing don't have any wants, the conversations end up just being about random things or people that aren't in the room. Those conversations are like awkward small talk – we do it just to do it. The next step up from a three-line conversation with a who and a where includes the addition of wants. Both people need to want something, whether it be tangible, like a cookie or sandwich, or intangible, like affirmation, attention, affection. Then they need to fight for what they want, thinking just like that kid in a grocery store.

Let's go back to the mom and child that wanted to borrow the car from the very first three-line example. Adding in the idea of wants, perhaps the mom wants the child to take on more responsibility and the child wants to be independent. The conversation then becomes about a bargain: you can have the car if you do the dishes every night or pay for gas. Maybe the child responds with the counter offer of showing independence by saying she isn't eating at home or she's making her own food and claiming to be an adult, so she doesn't have to do dishes. It's a simple example that makes the point, because the want moves the conversation and relationship forward. Both people are fighting for what they want, listening to one another, and they have a purpose for the conversation, all because they know what they want.

Now let's focus back on life, specifically interactions when we don't listen because we are so caught up in what 'needs' to be said. Think of the interview where you just wanted to tell the interviewer about this incredible thing that makes you the best candidate, so you just blurted it out at the most uncomfortable time, making an awkward moment. Or what about the date where you experienced word-vomit because you wanted to tell the other person about your day? How about the meeting where you had such an incredible point to make, never mind that someone made the exact point three points ago, and you blurted it out anyway, realizing it after the fact when no one responded to your amazing insight. Now, consider these three interactions with the addition of active listening AND knowing what you want. The interview: you work it into a question about your past employment. The date: you casually insert your cool day into a moment about how great Fridays are. The meeting: you actually listen to what's happening, and after the point gets made, you agree it's a great idea, and then you add more information or specifics to the original point.

What happens when you aren't sure about what you want? As mentioned earlier, in improv conversations when people don't know what they want, the conversation goes nowhere. In life, when people don't know what they want, they float. We've all experienced times in our lives when our wants weren't quite clear. I remember specifically when that happened for me. I was just about finished with school for the second time with another liberal art focus. I had a freelance job at a museum that I liked, an apartment in Brooklyn that was ok, a relationship that was most definitely best categorized as settling. I was fine – not great, not bad, just fine, and I had no idea how to be happier. I distinctly remember having a conversation with a friend after work and noticing everyone around me just seemed fine; no one was terribly happy or excited about what they were doing or where they were headed. It's a moment I think a lot of people hit in their late twenties and early thirties, and I'm told again in their late thirties, late forties, late fifties and so on. It's that moment of 'What am I doing?' Only then I didn't know how to fix it, or even improve it, so I just continued to float along, just fine, until I was trolling through Facebook and saw a post by my old improv theater. I thought about how happy I was doing improv, and at the same time how my museum job jokingly called me a 'show pony,' trotted out for important situations where a cool head and flexible nature were required. This wasn't because I was the best educator or some business like that; it was because I was seen as unflappable.

I didn't necessarily totally agree with the unflappable diagnosis; in those situations, I focused on my goal and what I needed to do to accomplish it. I didn't care who was observing my program and watching it from the outside. It didn't matter. What mattered were the students that were actively participating in the group. They were my 'real' audience, not the voyeurs on the outside simply watching what I did. My focus was always on my audience, what they needed and how I could reach them. Back to my happiness with improv: the only reason I left my team was school. At that point, it didn't matter that I didn't plan on being an actor; improv gave me a happiness high. Maybe I could go back. I was just floating anyway; why not add something to my schedule to change things up? In an impulsive moment when I should have been working on a resume or looking for a full-time job, I emailed the director and was back on stage the next week.

My return to improv quickly became more than just something to do. I went back and suddenly I saw where my unflappable nature came from, and that I actually WAS unflappable. It was wholly apparent that my hyper-focus, careful and sometimes intense listening skills, and flexibility in accomplishing goals came from my years of improv. I saw what made me successful in those 'show pony' situations. And as I said before, if you walk into an improv conversation with no idea what you want, the conversation goes nowhere. That was why my life felt like it was just progressing without direction, because I had no idea what I wanted. Like the ever-educator I am, I realized I could start teaching my museum coworkers how to use improv to become unflappable too! And right there, in my stagnant existence, I realized what I wanted and started working towards the idea of teaching improv to non-actors, no matter what it took.

Sounds like a happily ever after self-congratulating moment, huh? Improv will save you!

HA. Life at the point changed. It didn't, and hasn't, been easy. Plus, I already said this book wouldn't make you perfect. Practice doesn't make you perfect, it makes you better.

If you don't know what you want, you'll never progress. If you can't put what you want into very specific words, you'll cruise along and the conversation that is your life will read much like a 'fine' book or movie script; nothing special, nothing terrible. You might be reading this saying 'well that's all fine if you know what you want, what about those of us who have no idea what we want?!' Never fear! Improv is here!

I figured out what I wanted quickly because I had a bit of it before. Improv made me and still makes me feel free and happy. The moment I figured out that one life box, what I wanted to do when I grew up, everything else got clearer. I got out of that fine relationship and made my apartment nicer. Years later I figured out what I wanted in a relationship and how (and where) I wanted to live. It all started and developed with improv-based thinking.

Try This

If you are figuring out what you want in life, this is the activity for you. Write down the categories of your life that make you feel 'lost'. Some suggestions: Career, Health, Relationships/Family, Social/Fun, Money, Living Situation. Pick one area to focus on. This should be the area that you want to take action in first. Write that category on the top of a piece of paper and turn on a timer, your phone timer will do, for anywhere from five to ten minutes. Go at least five, no more than ten. Hit start and just write for the full time. Start listing or writing stream of consciousness or drawing or anything that helps you to get ideas down on paper, focusing on what you want in that category. Take my career example from earlier and I might write about how I wanted more freedom, affirmation for what I did, maybe something about being creative, a sentence on teaching, and a point about the ability to make a difference. For lack of a better phrase, you want to do a full-on brain dump. The only rule on day one? You have to write for at least five minutes and no more than ten. The five minutes are enough to get you moving and more than ten will get you in your head.

After you finish your full time, no cheating with only writing for a few minutes and then hopping on Facebook, put it away until tomorrow. Don't read it; don't fret over it, just sleep on it and walk away. The next day, set your timer for five to ten minutes. This time, read what you wrote, edit if necessary, and then add to it. After your time is up, put it away and leave it alone. Do the same on day three, four, five and six: read, edit, add and leave it alone. On day seven, look at the things that made it through the week. Those are the sticky things that you want.

A bit more on the why behind the timing and repetition for this activity: five minutes is long enough to get you thinking and too short to really stress you out. Five minutes is an easy amount of time; you probably spent five minutes (or more) checking social media this morning. When you are editing and adding, you could agonize for hours over what you want, which is why it's limited to ten minutes. You might not get through the whole thing in one day. That's ok! Still stop at ten minutes. You might not feel like writing. That's also ok! Just do five minutes. That's all you need because you are doing this for a few days.

Now that you have a list of wants, select ONE and think about how you can make it happen. Did you start laughing and put the book down yet? Don't! Brainstorm solutions as if you couldn't fail. You can't fail in improv – you're the best at whatever you do! Taking my earlier example, maybe my solution to wanting more freedom could be 'make my own schedule' or 'work whenever I want to'. Don't worry about logistics or the realism of the proposed solutions. Just brainstorm a list of possibilities, knowing the sky is the limit.

After you've brainstormed, look at your solutions. I'd be willing to bet they aren't all impossible and the ones that you initially thought were far-fetched are actually quite doable with time, work, and resources. When you take away the idea and possibility of failure, you get a few crazy ideas, and for the most part you get creative ideas that need some assistance. Now, take one of the solutions and break it up into bite-sized pieces and actions. Break tasks down as small as you need to in order to make the larger task doable. Think of the larger task as the fabric on an umbrella. It's held up by spokes – choices and actions – and it needs all of the spokes to maintain a useful shape. If the umbrella task is 'get a new job', the smaller spokes might be updating your resume, polishing your LinkedIn, and going to a networking event.

Focus on heading down the rabbit hole with your seed ideas. Follow them and don't find additional problems, just focus on ways to make them happen. Avoid any words or thoughts like 'I can't do that' or 'I don't know' or 'that won't work'. The only can't is that you can't fail.

The next step is the leap. Try to accomplish one of those spokes. You might fail. If you do, get up and do it again. If you fail again, try something different. You now have a plan! You know what you want, and you are trying to make your want a reality. You are further ahead than you were last week when you were probably grumbling about writing for five minutes. Celebrate the little wins. Negativity sticks, so when you have even the smallest victory, you shouldn't just brush it off. You need to take the positive, bask in it, and keep going.

Don't get discouraged if this is a difficult task. Wants in improv conversations are really difficult – and those aren't even real! Wants in real life? Harder. Start small and build. And remember: you can't fail.

Yes, And vs Yes, But

'Yes, And' is a way of life. It's probably one of the most referenced of all improv ideas in the professional non-actor world. There are multiple books, articles, podcasts, videos, memes, gifs and more from improv professionals that attempt to show how incredible Yes, And really is. It's also the most misused and misunderstood improv concept. In my opinion, and I think all of improv is pretty spectacular for personal growth, Yes, And is the most effective part of improv for people that want to see immediate results. While you'll start to feel the effects of active listening quickly, it is a skill that needs to develop over time. With Yes, And, you'll start to feel the effects immediately.

Yes, And sounds simple, and it is. It's also very complex. Yes, And is focused on affirming and then elevating or adding information. **It is not about agreeing with everyone and always saying yes.** This is not going to turn you into a 'Yes Person' who spreads themselves too thin and can't devote proper time to important things. This Yes is much more than just a normal agreeable yes.

Let's break down the Yes first. When you say Yes in Yes, And, you are agreeing to the reality, whether that be a situation, an opinion, a possibility or a thought. In an improv conversation, if I say the sky is blue, the sky is blue. If I say it is green, then it's green, unless we had already talked about and determined the color of the sky as something other than green. We agree with the reality of the situation. Revisiting those three-line conversations, if I say the first line and call you mom, then you are my mom in that conversation.

The 'wrong' way to respond to this would be saying, 'I'm not your mom, I'm your (insert another relationship that is not mom).' You've negated my idea of reality and stopped the conversation because now I'm either crazy or on something, and we're probably just going to awkwardly argue about our relationship. The nuance here is if I make a statement or ask you a question in an improv scene, you don't have to say yes to the mundane question or agree with ME, just the reality. If I ask 'do you want to go to the grocery store' you can easily say 'no I would rather not.' If I say 'I need to go to the grocery store' it's not effective to say 'there is no store, we're in space, what are you talking about?' Unless a store-less space has already been established, your contribution has halted the conversation because all that's left to do is argue about the reality of the situation or force someone to back down from a choice. Your job is to Yes the reality that gets created. In real life, you wouldn't necessarily argue with someone about what year it is. Same thing.

Because that's insanely wordy and complex, reread that paragraph if necessary, and don't feel badly if you are still a little confused. We've been conditioned that yes is all about agreeing with people, positivity, and going along with everything – and here, it's about agreeing with a reality.

Now let's focus on the And. With the And, you are elevating and/ or adding information to the reality that has been established. If we go back to my green sky example, I might say the sky is green and you might add, 'and the clouds are purple.' You've added something to the situation. You could also elevate what I said and reply with, 'and the green looks scary, I think a storm is coming!' That statement elevates the information and the reality. Tina Fey gives the best example in her book *Bossypants* regarding the nuance of Yes, And. Say you're part of an improv conversation, and someone walks up to you and says 'stick 'em up!' and holds their hand like a gun. A negation of reality would be, 'That's not a gun, that's your hand.'

With this response, you've ended the conversation, negated the idea and stopped the other person from moving forward. The Yes might sound like 'oh no! Take my money!' You've agreed to the situation and added nothing. The Yes, And response would be 'Oh no! And the gun I gave you for Christmas! You bastard!' The Yes, And not only affirms the reality, it also elevates the idea and adds information.

In improv conversations, the exact words of 'Yes, And' aren't often used. Most of the time, it's implied rather than stated. The above example from Tina Fey doesn't use the words; rather the idea is incorporated into the conversation. When people are learning how to Yes, And in improv OR life, I always advise them to be very deliberate and very contrived. Use the exact words until they are clearly implied. It's like the difference between hearing and listening; you need to make a conscious choice until it's automatically there.

Try This

Have a conversation with someone using the idea of Yes, And in your responses. You can either tell them that you are doing this, or let them figure it out on their own. Perhaps you are talking about the weather. It might sound like:

Other person: It's really nice outside today!
You: Yes, And I hope it stays like this for a while.
Other person: Well it's almost Spring, so we might be lucky!
You: Yes, And Spring is my second favorite time of year. I'm partial to fall.

While you might look and sound a little contrived at first, that Yes, And pushes a conversation forward. It allows for openness and further discussion.

The opposite of And is 'But'. In most conversations, the word But is overused and unnecessary. I've been thinking that the only reason you might want to use the word But is to pit two things against one another for an argument. Think about it, what does the word But do that the word And can't? Imagine the same conversation in the activity above, and substitute And with But. It might go something like this:

Other person: It's really nice outside today.
You: Yes, but I hope it stays like this for a while.
Other person: Well, it's almost Spring, so we might be lucky!
You: Yes, but Spring is my second favorite time of year, I'm partial to fall.

The person playing the part of 'You' in this situation? That person looks like the ultimate Debbie Downer. The word But puts a damper on this particular conversation and makes it negative. While it's different than the negation of insisting the gun in Tina Fey's example is just a hand, it still halts the conversation.

But isn't just detrimental because it makes a person or situation negative. The word But in conversation also tends to elevate one idea over another or stages one idea against another. In language, we use But for several reasons. We've got the conjunction – something that contrasts; the preposition – in place of except; and the adverb – in place of only. In conversation, we use it most often as a conjunction and preposition. Is it really necessary though? Just as we're told to replace our 'I thinks' and 'I feels' with declarative statements because they sound stronger, why can't we replace our Buts with Ands whenever we can to sound less combative? Imagine this professional situation:

Person 1: I really think we could try to plan ahead for programs.
Person 2: But that's not how we work around here.

Unfortunately, I've heard this interaction more than once – even when I come in as a consultant to try to help people plan ahead! The result of this But is a self-elevation of Person 2, and a dismissal of Person 1's ideas. By Person 2 saying But to start their sentence, they've declared in one word that they are the expert in the situation. They know better. Unless Person 1 decides to argue the point, the conversation stalls. Let's look at the same conversation with a substitution of And:

Person 1: I really think we could try to plan ahead for programs.
Person 2: And that's not how we work around here.

Awkward and snarky, right? Now let's see what it looks like with a Yes, And, as well as a request for more information:

Person 1: I really think we could try to plan ahead for programs.
Person 2: Yes, and that's not how we work around here. Can we discuss your ideas?

This interaction, while semi-contrived by placing Yes, And in front of a declarative statement, asks for more information naturally. If you simply added the request for more information to the original conversation, that But still stops the conversation:

Person 1: I really think we could try to plan ahead for programs.
Person 2: But that's not how we work around here. Can we discuss your ideas?

The But is dismissive of the request and the ask for additional information seems like a 'must do' instead of a 'want to do' for open communication. Now let's look at the same interaction with Yes, And used as an affirmation and elevation:

Person 1: I really think we could try to plan ahead for programs.

Person 2: Yes, you think we could try to plan ahead for programs, and that's not how we work around here. Let's talk about it.

This time, the Yes, And affirms what the other person is thinking, adds another opinion, and elevates the conversation by making an offer to continue the discussion. This style of communication eliminates the confrontational nature of But, and also opens up a further discussion with the other person. Remember, the word But not only shuts down a conversation, it also opens a confrontation. When used a conjunction, But is meant to present something that contrasts, and contrasting points often lead to arguments. The goal of an argument is for someone to win – which is NOT the point of a discussion. The goal of a discussion is to simply break down ideas. Many improv arguments end up running in circles until someone ends the cycle. The same is true with many real life arguments. This isn't to say we should always agree. A contrasting point can be established without the confrontation by using the word And. You can present an additional viewpoint that conflicts, and you can keep the conversation moving and open-ended. Furthermore, And is synonymous with an equal sign. My opinion is no better than yours. You are more than welcome to hate something I love, and I'm more than welcome to love something you hate. We're not better than each other, we are equals. Yes, And keeps conversations flowing because no one feels as though their opinion doesn't matter or is less important than someone else's.

Try This

Find another person and have a Yes, And conversation about an object. Maybe you look at a wall or something from your bag or something in the fridge. In order to model this activity, let's say we are looking at a cupcake. One person will start and notice something about the cupcake, and the other person will affirm what was said and add information to elevate the observation. The conversation might sound like:

Person 1: I see frosting.
Person 2: Yes, you see frosting And I see sprinkles.

One of the critical ideas behind this activity concerns the exact repeat of the other person. Don't paraphrase, don't add additional meaning and don't change anything. With the Yes, you aren't adding your opinion, you are affirming theirs. The activity might continue on like:

Person 1: Yes, you see sprinkles And I see a wrapper.
Person 2: Yes, you see a wrapper And I see crumbs.

This isn't a memory game. It's only to practice the use of Yes, And. You aren't remembering and repeating everything that has been said. Once the use of Yes, And is practiced and easier than it was when you started, switch over to 'I think' instead of 'I see'. The conversation might sound like:

Person 1: I think cupcakes are delicious.
Person 2: Yes, you think cupcakes are delicious And I think they are too sugary.
Person 1: Yes, you think they are too sugary And I think it's ok to splurge every now and then.
Person 2: Yes, you think it's ok to splurge every now and then And I think cupcakes are out of style and overdone.

The above example purposely shows different opinions. Your opinion can be the same or different. You should be listening, responding authentically, and using the Yes, And to build the conversation. Stay on topic, whatever that might be, even if it gets difficult. You might be thinking how easy this sounds. Cupcakes are a lot easier to talk about than say, work or politics. Establish the pattern with easy topics, and then try to apply it to a difficult situation. Imagine this tactic with a work-related issue:

Person A: I need a raise!
Person B: Yes, I hear you need a raise and we don't have the money right now. Can we think about future options?

Boom. The situation gets diffused because the person is affirmed and heard – the repeat does that naturally. Information is added, with a request to extend the conversation. The only hazard in this activity and using Yes, And in life? You have to be ready for more conversation. It's not something that is going to shut people down, it's something that is going to open people up. And the active listening that you're developing? Major workout with Yes, And.

Yes, And isn't just used for conversation, it's also a great way to work on team brainstorming. Maybe you are thinking about a new idea or initiative at work. The Yes, And in this next activity is used to elevate ideas and creatively brainstorm. The best part of this activity? You can't fail. If this is a struggle, and it is for most people, you should constantly remind yourself that in improv-thinking, the only failure is sitting back and doing nothing at all or saying 'I can't' when you <u>want</u> to do something. With that in mind, when you are adding information in a Yes, And brainstorm, you can add anything. Nothing is impossible. Let's go back to that cupcake:

Person 1: I have a great idea for a cupcake. It's going to have the best frosting.
Person 2: Yes, and that frosting will be the delicious kind, not the gritty kind.
Person 1: Yes, and that delicious frosting will be available in any flavor.
Person 2: Yes, and those flavors will be all natural.

The additional information elevates a component of the last comment. Essentially, the idea is being refined further and further, focusing in on a bigger and more creative picture. Try this tactic in your next meeting. Instead of waiting for the opportunity to say your idea or contribution, try to focus on elevating the current idea. That might include parts of your original idea and it might include a totally new idea!

Bonus Round: Empathy!

While empathy should be a part of life and not just a bonus, sometimes we need to work on our communication of empathy. Yes, And automatically infuses you with a forced empathy – you have to listen to what the other person says, affirm that they do indeed feel this way, and add information to what they said. That validation of opinion is a key part of actively showing empathy, and can lead to a greater understanding of others and their perspective.

Cautions of Yes, And

I love Yes, And. I even have it tattooed on my arm in my husband's handwriting because I feel so strongly about the idea of affirmation and elevation in good communication, conversation and life. What other phrase can make people feel empowered, allow them to realize that their ideas are worthwhile, AND help you listen and communicate on a higher and more empathetic level? With all its magic, I also admit that it can be used incorrectly, and I've often seen it misunderstood and used as a throwaway statement or qualifier. I now present the major cautions of Yes, And.

The first caution has been expressed a few times already: be sure to understand what you are affirming. If you are using the technique of repeating what just got said, be sure to repeat it word for word. If you are Yes, Anding an idea and have moved past the repeat, be sure you aren't interpreting the information and taking too many liberties with someone else's statement and idea. If you are saying Yes, and then you change what got said or the meaning behind what got said, all you are doing is going back to agenda-orientated thinking. You aren't meant to interpret what's been said or how someone feels or what they think; you're affirming it. Yes, they said this, Yes, they feel this, Yes, they think this. Remember you don't have to agree, you need to affirm that this is indeed what they see, think, say, feel, etc. You are affirming THEM and their statement, not your opinion of the statement. Empathy comes into play here as well – you are seeking to understand where they are coming from. You aren't fighting or trying to convince them of your beliefs or validating yourself. Remember – affirm.

Be sure to actively listen and pay attention to what is being said. Focus on the words that are coming out of your mouth as much as the words that are coming out of their mouth. Recently, I was working at a leadership institute teaching an EE workshop, and a few faculty members told me that a well-known improv theater came to lead workshops a few years ago, and they also taught Yes, And. It was no surprise to hear the leadership staff was misusing Yes, And. They told me the well-known improv theater did not emphasize the base ideas of affirmation and elevation crucial to understanding Yes, And.

Some people at the institute had turned into 'Yes People'. I briefly touched on this before, and it stands to reiterate: You don't need to say yes to everything. I'm sure my fellow coaches are cringing, so hear me out. If you say yes to everything always, you will spread yourself too thin. If you are trying out positive risk taking for a day, a week, a month – great. Set an end time. Do not live life saying yes to everything. You'll neglect things like your social life, your career, your health – you can't do everything! If you are following everyone else with a Yes, what are **you** working towards? What do you want? Do not misinterpret Yes, And as turning into a follower that doesn't have an original thought. These Yes People were agreeing to everything, even things they didn't believe in one bit! You don't have to change who you are. You're just communicating in a more open and empathetic style.

Other people at the institute were using Yes, And as a throwaway. They learned that it opened communication, and didn't understand exactly how it opened communication. Conversations would start and someone would say 'Yes, and I don't think this will work' without even stopping to listen to what had been said. That whole activity about noticing observations and Yes, Anding a partner using their exact words? There's a point to the repetition. You're not just using the words to use the words, you are using the Yes to specifically affirm what they see, and the And to specifically elevate and add. They aren't throwaway filler words – they have meaning. It's why I start people on that very simple and contrived activity. It develops a habit of Yes, And that leads to a mastery of the phrase AND the meaning behind it.

Keeping these cautions in mind, Yes, And is a powerful addition to your communication skills. Follow the pattern: affirm, repeat what has been said, and add your information to the conversation, and you'll see how quickly Yes, And improves your conversations and communication style. Don't forget the simple word Yes – it is incredibly empowering to affirm and be affirmed. Both words are imperative to the success of Yes, And. Apologies in advance, most of my students also lament that after learning about Yes, And, they hear Buts all the time. Pay attention if that's you with all the Buts or if it's someone else, and try to insert a Yes, And where you can. If you are dealing with people that are constantly saying But, you can try first to lead by example, and then next hand them this book, or (better yet) try being transparent that their use of But is halting conversations and elevating their opinions over others. Most people aren't malicious.

When laying out the information in this book, I struggled with what was **most** important – I made arguments and edited more times than I care to admit. I knew that the last section about self was going to be the last section – when we start delving into finding our authentic selves, it can get a little stressful and a little emotional. Which is another reason why I saved the last caution with Yes, And for this transitional moment. Communication and Social Communication are two different things. While they both involve the same basic skills, self-awareness and reflection are gigantic. Why we say the things we say, and why we choose the 'how' behind what we say can be a book in itself. The awareness that connects with the focus of And in Yes, And instead of But straddles the line with communication and social skills.

Think of the last time you used the word But – were you making a statement and you added a But afterwards? I hear this a lot:

*I think that we should [insert idea here] **But** we could also [insert another idea here].*

The above statement can be made up of any two ideas and your audience can be personal, professional, family, anything. That But puts more value on the second part of your statement and negates the first. Why say But? Why value one above another or argue with yourself?

You might want to offer two ideas. Why can't you say, 'I think that we should [idea] And we could also [second idea]'? Means the same.

You might not be completely sure about your ideas. You've already said, 'I think…' which means you believe in it – which you do, right?

Or you might be offering that second statement as a safety blanket. 'I think that we should [idea] But we could also [second idea].'

Translation: Here's my first idea that I really like and I'm going to give you a second idea just in case you don't like this first idea.

Not ok, friends.

Remember what the word But does – it elevates an idea above another, it pits two ideas against one another, and it discounts the first statement. Unless you are very specifically choosing to do one of those things, why use it?

And when you start thinking about what your words mean, and their intention, start looking inside. Why offer two ideas? If you really want opinions on both, awesome! If they are equally important, make sure that's understood. If you need a safety blanket – why? What's going on in the situation that makes you lose confidence? Or is this you, all the time, because something ELSE is making you nervous? Have a check in moment and think about what's going on. And if this terrifies you, or you don't really know how to do this, don't worry. I got you.

Let's dive into awareness, shall we?

Finding Yourself

Welcome! You made it to the most complicated and difficult section of this book. If you skipped right to this section or saw one of the numerous prompts directing you here, hello! In my years of teaching improv to non-actors, more often than not students have some kind of self-awareness moment that scares the daylights out of them. It might be during class, it might be after class, it might be a few weeks or months down the line. Whatever the situation, the preparation for life that happens with improv for non-actors causes a long hard look at social communication and personal relationships. Remember, improv is simply heightened reality. You are yourself. You can practice making new, stronger and bolder choices, and you are still yourself and will still act in a way that is uniquely YOU. Even if you are playing a 'crazy' and unrealistic character in class, or embracing the play-based learning that comes with improv, you will always be you.

Social communication is one of the most nuanced and rewarding parts of improvement through improv. People can get by with their general communication skills being a bit scripted, and public speaking and presentation skills can be a mindset that can get slipped on and off. Social communication is a life change. Research shows it takes us up to 21 days for a simple task to become a habit, and more complex tasks take up to 66 days. Life changes take time! There are so many facets that make you YOU, and when you're working on yourself, the big list of changes can seem incredibly daunting. I need to stop saying Um. I need to be more direct. I need to take initiative. I need to [insert years of professional and personal development here]. Remember, practice doesn't make you perfect – it makes you better.

Social communication is focused on bettering <u>yourself</u>, and since self-improvement and communication are huge topics, it helps to break things down. You're going to the gym for your SELF – your brain, your psyche, your emotions. Work on tiny tasks every day and you'll feel improvement. Promise. Baby steps forward are still moving forward. Falling flat on your face and getting up? You are still moving forward.

In class and coaching, I tell students they can be themselves or they can be someone else when we are doing activities. It really doesn't matter to the conversation or to classwork. You still have to pay attention to the reality that is being created, listen to your partner(s) and affirm and elevate information. You could be a talking dog or a lawyer (and I've even seen lawyers play talking dogs – never the other way around...) The persona that is being placed on top of YOU is still YOU – it's just like wearing a different outfit when you meet with coworkers instead of Sunday comfy clothes. The trick to picking the 'right' way for you to learn the most about yourself? Try lots of different ways and see how you feel.

Recently, I saw the difference between being yourself and being someone else. A gentleman, who identified as an entrepreneur, had a three-line conversation in week one where he pretended to be someone else. He commented that it felt a lot like acting and was very freeing and fun. I think the best way he described it was by saying he felt he could 'do whatever he wanted', which is a common feeling in improv. The next week, he was part of a longer conversation where the other individual initiated, setting up the who and where, and it happened to be a situation he had experienced in real life, unbeknownst to his partner. His partner was playing a female employee asking for a raise, and he talked around her and her request the entire time. We moved into reflection and he said 'this felt more like role-play than improv, I was just myself.' The thing is, he chose to be himself in that moment. He could have responded in any possible way, and because it was so close to what happened that very morning, he responded in the very same way he did earlier that day – he avoided her request and talked her into a confusing circle.

Why did that happen? When people are involved in conversations that resemble things they experience every day, they tend to fall into their every day habits. Turns out, this particular gentleman tended to fall into conflict avoidance when he was in work situations, and the woman he was working with also happened to avoid direct conflict. She let herself get talked into a corner where she either had to directly ask for what she wanted (not her thing) or just accept that she wasn't going to get him to give her a raise.

I stopped and asked them to run through the same situation again. One of the beautiful parts of improv – you can always get a redo. Only this time, I suggested they try to fight for what they want. I told the man to think about what he wanted, and move forward. I told the woman to try different tactics – do something that causes a little discomfort. Maybe be incredibly direct. Maybe try being completely off the wall and threaten him for a raise – not something I suggest in real life! It's fun to try things on for size when there are no real consequences. They reset and redid the conversation – and the man kept trying to avoid the woman's requests (because, as we heard later, he didn't want to give her a raise), and the woman was trying to get him to address the raise. A few moments went by, and finally, she demanded it. She became very confrontational, citing instances where she did his work, and finally, he gave in – flustered. She was someone other than herself – someone that was incredibly confrontational and direct. When we reflected, she said it felt great to be direct and ask for what she wanted. He said he was incredibly uncomfortable because he didn't have any control in the situation.

And there it is – heightened reality and an extension to who we are every day.

This reality just so happened to be close to what their real life WAS. Sure, the reality can be completely crazy town and you could have a talking dog and cat or a world where someone happens to be a surgeon with old school fishing materials, and that's perfectly acceptable. The point is, it's a reality and you'll be an extension of who you are. We might be starting from nothing in improv – we are also influenced by all of our experiences in life. We are the sum of our parts, and no matter what, that comes out.

So how can you take every day situations and 'fix' them with improv? As I am writing this, just today, I was teaching a group of women writers. We were doing an improv activity that required four people, and she was in a group with three very strong personalities – and they all started bossing her around and saying she wasn't good at her job. She got so caught up that even though it was essentially 'make believe', she had started to cry – it was too much like real life for her, she admitted later, with people bullying her and trying to push her into making a choice. I asked her why she didn't just yell back at them, or tell them to knock it off. Her answer was telling:

I didn't know I could.

My response? *Who says you can't?*

Before addressing the example directly, think about the last time you said that you 'can't' do something. I'm not talking about the times you said no to plans or something you really didn't want to do – I'm talking about those times that you really want something and you come out with a regretful 'oh I can't' or the times at work when someone proposes an idea, and you respond with 'oh we can't' – or someone says that to you without any explanation. Maybe you're thinking it right now with something that's happening in your life. Now, examine the situation and think about why you can't. Is it because it's against the law? Against your values or moral obligations to the world? Because you don't currently have the means?

Or because you just don't think you can?

Sure, the woman from the earlier example can't yell back at her coworkers during the day. Well, she shouldn't. She can practice standing up for herself if that happens again in class. She can, in her own way, tell them to cool it. Or she could tell them to cool it in not-her-own-way. Time to try something new! The best part? She can flip out in class if she wants to. She can yell, she can name call, she can pull out the most unprofessional self that she can possibly muster – and she can see what happens next. And if it fails? Nothing happens, because it's improv class. She also might find some confidence in that bold behavior. And what if she tells them to cool it in real life and it fails? She's working on standing up for herself and speaking up.

Finding yourself is an adventure. It's also one of the reasons I don't want to ever do any kind of performance with our students. When you perform, even improv, there's a finality that happens. You do a show, the audience claps when it's over. The End! Applause!

Improv is worth so much more when you focus on the learning process, not the finality of a show. Learning and growth are worth so much more when they are a regular part of your life instead of focused on a test or a whack-a-mole situation where you're fixing the things that pop up.

Finding yourself is never finished; so don't look to the end. If you focus on the process, progress and growth, you'll keep finding yourself instead of pretending that you've been found.

Show, Don't Tell

In improv, people don't talk about what they are going to do, they do it. You show what you are doing. One of my favorite Tina Fey quotes sums up this idea perfectly: 'You can't be that kid standing at the top of the waterslide, overthinking it. You have to go down the chute.' Things HAPPEN in improv. The moment you start talking about doing something, you need to go ahead and do it. If you're blocking the slide, not only are you stuck, people around you just want you to move. Eventually, they'll get tired of waiting and go around. Heading down the slide isn't <u>just</u> for the people behind you. It's for you too.

How can we embrace that mentality in real life? Considering the earlier example of the woman being bossed around, one of the things she said through tears was that she really wanted to tell the bullies that kept telling her what to do to knock it off, and she could never find the right time to do it. This was for the class conversation, and life was even worse! It was always too busy or there were too many people around or it was too late or another person was right there. She said she was planning to wait for the right time. Her reasoning was full of things she wanted to do 'one day' and reasons why she couldn't do it. The next time she was up with one of the people from the original group, something different happened without my coaching. Again, the other person was driving the conversation. This time, the woman that was getting bossed around finally just yelled 'STOP TALKING!' and everyone froze. I don't think the rest of the class believed that she had it in her – I did, because everyone does – and they just kind of looked at her. Afterward, in reflection,

I asked her how that felt to finally yell and let it go on her own, and she replied, 'Awesome!' She stopped waiting for the right time, didn't make an excuse and just did it. Will this transfer to life? Hope so. Because I know she can.

Try This

Action is hard to take. It's simple to talk about the things we want to do and think about those earlier mentioned 'can'ts' and 'shouldn'ts'. Taking initiative is extra hard if you aren't used to taking action on a semi-regular basis. And when you are starting from the place we do in improv-based conversations, it's almost crippling with all of the creativity and possible outcomes!

What if for one single day, you focused on being completely action-orientated? Instead of thinking about what you want to do in that moment, focus on what you can do immediately. These action items can be as small or as large as you want! Stop talking about looking for a new job – make or refresh your resume. Don't keep fretting about being single. Join a dating site and go on a date. Quit lamenting about being stuck in your life, change something. Remember to reflect after this action-orientated day, and see what happens!

Mindfulness + Self-Awareness

Every aspect of social communication starts with you. All too often, I ask a student specific details about the choices in their improv conversations and I'm greeted with an 'I don't know' or something that is gray instead of black and white. In improv conversations, the specific details are crucial. In order to move conversations forward, you need to know Who you are, Where you are and what you Want. When we also think about our emotions and how we feel in a situation, we get even more clarity on how to move a conversation and moment forward.

Think about the last memorable conversation you had. Where were you? What was your relationship with the person you were talking to? What did you want out of the conversation? And how did you feel during? How about after?

The bigger question: were you even aware of how you felt?

I've heard mindfulness and self-awareness used interchangeably with my students. Mindfulness is attention to the present. Self-awareness is the understanding of how you react and respond in the present. They go hand in hand, as you can't be attentive to the moment without being aware of how you attend to the present, and it's impossible to be aware of how you attend to the present if you are never ACTUALLY in the moment. While this sounds a bit like the connection between listening and hearing, and that attention to yourself is a choice, much of the understanding of self-awareness and mindfulness comes from reflection. Whenever people ask me how to develop self-awareness and mindfulness outside of the improv classroom, my go to advice is always the same: step back, look at the situation and reflect. That last memorable conversation? Reflect on it. And on the next one. And the one after that. This reflective habit comes naturally in EE's practice of improv because you're existing in a space where a bunch of voyeurs are watching you have an important moment, only you aren't actively acknowledging the 'watchers' until you reflect on the situation. In life, we usually don't have an audience for our private important moments – in improv, you are the 'show'.

A great example of awareness and mindfulness from came from a class I teach at a local college. Two students had a clear relationship, a clear location and each of them wanted something. They were husband and wife, they were in the kitchen, he wanted her to pay attention to him when he got home from work and she wanted a compliment. The woman focused on her want so much that she moved away from her normal 'self', which is an independent and fierce feminist. She transformed to a husband appeasing and smiling Stepford-like wife, holding that persona through his misogyny just to get what she wanted. He maintained who he is, and got his attention. He pushed his want more than she did, and finally near the end, she got her compliment by appeasing him even more. The class applauded, and we reflected on what happened. The woman immediately confessed that she felt gross being that far away from her norm. This woman, unbeknownst to us before and admitted by her during the reflection, wanted to work on her confrontation skills in class. She felt she often emotionally snapped quickly when she wanted something, and this was her attempt to try a new tactic. While the woman knew that she wanted to work on being less of a fighter, she realized being the person that gives in and appeases all the time was something she didn't want at all. That feeling wasn't worth the result.

This example strikes me as such a fascinating moment in self-awareness, because she was not only visibly uncomfortable, which was apparent to everyone watching, she also took an immediate assessment of how she felt in that moment and shared it with the group. Have you heard of the idea if you don't say it, it isn't real? Once she said it out loud, she had an easier time processing that this was NOT what she wanted – she had to find an internal compromise. She was comfortable admitting that she didn't like fighting all the time, and disliked the other end even more. That honesty with yourself is something we should all strive for. We don't often check in with how we feel in situations, and rarely get the opportunity to reflect afterwards because we are already on to the next moment.

We get asked 'how are you?' all the time, and usually, we just gloss over the answer with a 'fine' or 'good' or some other bland answer that leads into another ask of 'how are you?' Are you honest with the person asking the question? Are you honest with yourself? If you aren't being truthful with yourself, you aren't being aware. If you aren't 'good' or 'fine' and you're just saying that you are because you really don't know how you are, stop. Check in. How are you really? Reflection, as mentioned in the beginning of this book, is crucial for growth. Don't keep living the same life hoping for something different to happen one of these times. Check in, reflect, plan, change. Self-reflection starts the trajectory for self-awareness.

It is ok to not be ok and admit when something is wrong. As self-aware as I am, I ignored a serious bout of depression that put me in a terrible place. I knew something was wrong, and then it would go away and I'd forget about it and move on. Only after a huge escalation did I reflect on why this was happening – and when I stepped back, I realized that it was happening every single month at the same time. A trip to the doctor and a lot of crying conversations later, I was diagnosed with PMDD (Premenstural dysphoric disorder) and severe depression. Even before that, I knew I wasn't ok. It was easier to ignore when it went away for my 'easy days' and just deal with it all over again when it kicked up.

This is a good time to connect directly back with improv. There are a lot of improv activities that embrace repetition, and a lot more that expose the patterns in our lives and in the lives of those around us. One of the best ways to see these patterns is to regularly check in with yourself **AND** the people around you. Ask those people if you have any behavioral patterns. In the next Try This, pay attention to habits and WHY you feel the way you do. Are there certain situations that cause you to behave in a certain way? If you are in a bad mood, do you get anxious? If you are happy, do you take more risks? Pay attention to your own behaviors and patterns – you won't see them until you pay attention.

The reason you need to pay attention to the people around you? People on the outside often see things first. Happens every time in class – people watching the conversation playing out on stage can see the woman trying the same tactic to get what she wants. They can see the man continuing to bargain, bargain, and bargain. Both of them think they are trying different things – they are saying different words, right? It's a new bargain! Ask your close friends and family if you have any patterns or expected behaviors. Do you cry when you're angry? Do you give up when you are frustrated?

When you take a breath, step back and look at these patterns, you can see if you are stuck in any hamster wheels of repetition. If you want to change, change. If the pattern works for you, keep it. For me, when someone says that I can't do something, I go out and do it. I'm comfortable with that pattern. My depression was another story. 20 days out of the month I was 'fine' and 10 were hell. That pattern had to be altered.

What do you need to step back, examine, and keep or change?

And how are you?

Try This

Right now, take note of how you feel. Put the book down and check in. Ask yourself 'Self, how are you right now?' and answer. Not the polite kind of answer of 'I'm fine!' The real and gritty answer that describes how you actually feel in this moment. Assign an emotion to it and make a note, either physically writing it down or mentally checking in. Set an alarm to check in again tomorrow morning, midday and tomorrow night. Then do it three times the next day, and the next day as well. The more you do this, the more you'll habitually check in with yourself. You don't need to share it with anyone; you just need to take the moment to think about and note how you feel. To the above point, think about patterns and repetition!

Why check in? Aside from awareness in the moment, knowing how you react to a situation and how you behave under certain conditions helps develop a greater understanding of how your emotions alter your actions. If you are unaware of how you feel in a given moment, you might be responding in a way that is either too emotionally charged or not emotionally checked in. One of the best improv activities for assessing emotional awareness is called 'Changing Emotions.' It starts with two people having a conversation. At any moment, the facilitator can call out ANY emotion. When an emotion is called, both people need to take on that emotion to its highest degree. The conversation ends up progressing much faster than it naturally would due to the heightened emotional state. Our emotions drive decision-making, relationship building, connection, and motivation. On the flip side, we sometimes shield our emotions and focus our decision making on logic. There are times when we simply have to be professional and maintain composure. The problems lie when we either let emotions control our actions and aren't aware of it, or we do things without connecting to how we feel about the situation. The truth is, we need both.

Think of the last time you were disrespected. Think about how the rest of the day was going before that happened and how you felt afterward. Were you already having a bad day? Did the rest of the day get worse? Did you just shake it off? Now think of the last time you were disrespectFUL. How was your day before you were disrespectful? How did you feel after? Unless you are some kind of malicious sociopath, which I'm sure you aren't, you probably had a really bad day before you were disrespectful. Did you know that you were going to be rude before it happened, or did you have a moment of regret after?

Now the bigger question: could it have been avoided if you just took note of your emotions BEFORE that moment and proceeded with caution?

Sometimes I think adults need to put themselves in a time out. As mentioned earlier, it's ok to be not ok. Since our emotions drive SO much, we have sayings like 'check it at the door' or what my mom always told me, 'find a tree to touch and leave your emotions before you go in to a situation'. While I recognize the value in this, it doesn't work for me. Not at all. I wear my emotions on my sleeve. I'm sure the same is true for many of you – the way to best be yourself in the moment? Check yourself, not your emotions. Being aware of yourself, like if you get cranky when you're hangry or weepy when you're tired, helps you take a time out when necessary AND recognize that your decisions and interactions are connected to your emotions. If you can't take a time out, do something that brightens your mood. I'm food-driven, so I'll either promise myself a treat after or grab something before I do anything that requires me to be in a good mood, if I'm not in one already.

Thinking back to Changing Emotions, we usually don't operate life feeling everything at a level 10. What about the days that we do? What about those decisions we wish we wouldn't have made because they were colored by extreme emotion?

This is a good time to reveal a nuance within improv: it's more about responding than reacting. The trick is developing the mindfulness to take note of that awareness and remembering to step back, to see how you feel, and to respond with your state in mind instead of <u>just</u> reacting. Your response time simply speeds up.

Easy right? (HA!)

It's a wonder we get anything done with all of this back and forth, focus and self-awareness, wants and emotions. If you break things down into small pieces, growth and change become much easier and more manageable. In improv AND in real life, there are four things that a conversation requires: Who you are, Where you are, What you want and How you feel. Think of the last conversation you had in real life and answer these questions:

What is your relationship with this person?
Where are you?

Look! Two of the four necessary things for conversation in real life are simple! Now think about the next two:

What do you want from this conversation?
How do you feel?

If you didn't know what you wanted from the conversation, and it wasn't just a fun small talk conversation, it might have been a little frustrating. On the flip side, if you knew what you wanted and weren't sure how you felt, the situation was probably just as frustrating. Now think of a conversation or situation that you felt very strongly about. Why was the emotion so strong? Did you have a solid want? It might seem clinical to think of the four things – who, where, wants, emotion – as things and categories. That strong outcome or emotion was probably due to strength and specificity in the other areas.

Self-awareness is something that will build over time, and it will eventually lead to an acceptance of who you are. I can tell a lot about a person with just a few quick improv activities and it's pretty amazing watching someone discover something about themselves through improv. After you've checked in a few times with how you feel, think about how you'd answer the same 'How are you?' question if a coworker asked. How about a significant other? A family member? Would it be the same answer that you're giving yourself or would it be edited and filtered? This is where further reflection and an awareness of how you connect with the people around you come into play. If you know how you feel and choose to present a different self to the world, and those two are conflicting, you'll feel that internal conflict. Maybe you're already feeling it!

Before I left NYC for Winston-Salem, I noticed I was holding my breath every now and then at the weirdest times. I would be making dinner or driving to get coffee or brushing my teeth, and I would be holding my breath to the point I felt dizzy. As soon as I realized this, I started to check in while I was holding my breath. At the time, NYC was slowly killing me. I'm not being overdramatic here, I was slowly and surely being destroyed by the city and life I used to love so much. Now, I have a much different relationship with New York. I was doing things because I 'had' to. I was an actor, I HAVE to live in NYC. I was in museums, I HAVE to be in NYC. I own a business, I HAVE to stay in NYC.

I was presenting something that wasn't authentic. Even though I felt stressed, anxious and miserable, I wasn't sharing those emotions with the people in my life. It was taking the improv check in to heart that nurtured my self-awareness and relieved the conflict between what I felt and what I was putting out. When I took some time to check in, I realized that I wanted to succeed with EE more than I wanted to ever succeed with acting or museum work. I just didn't know what success looked like to me, and that was causing me so much anxiety. While I could coach people on discovering what success and failure meant to them, I was having a very hard time figuring out what it meant to me. Which leads to a bigger problem, especially with imposter syndrome and failure worry – if you don't know what success IS, how do you really know what a failure is? And worse, if you don't know what failure is, how could you fail?

It all changed when I took a breath (maybe the one I was holding?!) I started to figure out how I felt about life, and reflected on what I was putting out to others. I was high-level floating. Not getting by in a traditional sense. Just getting by in my own way, panicking when I was alone and putting on a good face to others, dealing with depression 10 days for every 30. I resolved this conflict with intense reflection and self check ins. I kept asking, why did I feel this way? I would take note of the answer, check in again, and take note of the answer. Rinse, wash, repeat. Finally, I realized that I was going through the same thing so many of our students were coming to us for! I was stuck in a hamster wheel of my own creation. I would run and run and run and still be in the same spot with my life and business. It turned out that life in NYC was at the root of a lot of problems, and the eventual solution was leave the city. I started exploring every business trip as a place to move. I asked myself, could I live here? When I opened up the opportunity to leave and didn't see NYC as my HAVE to, I met the guy who is now my husband. I met him in the unlikeliest of all places, Winston-Salem, NC. And after a few months of a long distance relationship, I took the biggest risk I had ever taken in my whole life and I decided to move to a place I had only visited, where I superficially knew a handful of people and was a complete departure from the last ten years of my life. I did what I had been urging my students to do in class and what I pushed friends to do. I did what I knew I sometimes tiptoed around both when I was onstage and in life. I did what Del Close, an improv great, always said. I followed the fear.

This personal story serves to show two things. The first deals with self-awareness and the connection between how you feel and what other people think you feel. It's not a given for anyone. I've been called 'unapologetically myself,' and I encourage students to be unapologetically their best selves. Even though I try to embody all of the things I teach – like confidence, I didn't always have the follow through. I didn't know how to take a risk that was ACTUALLY a risk for me, and I had developed some kind of comfort in stagnancy. The image of 'it's all fine' was all fine until it wasn't. The second links back to holding my breath. Are you fretting about something? Are you not breathing properly? If you aren't feeling yourself, it might be coming out in ways you'll see through checking in. Developing a regular habit of reflection on how you feel and why you feel that way helps you not only get where you want to go, it also communicates what you want and how you feel. That self-awareness, like listening, is a choice and a skill that builds up over time.

If you're beating yourself up right now or feeling like you don't know yourself, stop. You'd be surprised how many people aren't in tune with how they really feel or who they really are. All the 'be yourself' motivational language we got growing up? It's all ruined by high school, or college, or your first job, or your first break up. We're encouraged to be ourselves until that self hits a wall. So hit the reset button. Figure out yourself piece by piece and own it. When you are being your best self, that strong and specific YOU, you'll have that confidence when you walk into a room to speak. The black and white choices I told you to make in three line conversations? They help that specific activity for the same reason I'm telling you to define things in your life. Knowing yourself gives you power over anything.

Try This

Check in again. How are you? Take a deep breath and let it out. Put one hand on your stomach and the other on your lower back. Take another deep breath and make sure that you are filling your hands up with air. Now let it out. Take one more deep breath, filling your hands up with air, and let it out. Now check in again. Feel different? Deep breaths allow us to focus on the present and be fully in a moment. We spend so much time rushing around, heading to the next thing. Try to do this a few times a week when you need it and be sure to note how you feel.

Risk + Failure

When you get beyond the incredible opportunities for developing awareness and growing your communication skills, improv is about risk and failure. To reap the full benefits, you need to first master the basics. If you aren't listening to yourself and responding to your own needs, you can't understand what is a risk and what is a failure. On top of that, since failure is so personal, you need to understand yourself enough to figure out what constitutes a failure, which brings up the question: is anything a failure if we can identify it as a growth opportunity? And <u>can</u> you know success without knowing failure?

I've been touching on risk and failure throughout, and before I start getting completely cerebral, improv itself is a risk. Making the choice to learn improv, in class or through this book, is a risk. I tell students in class and in life, just go for it. If something doesn't work, who cares? In class, it's over after three minutes, and in life, your choices probably won't end in a life or death situation. The fear or trepidation usually happens when people are faced with taking initiative. I hear 'I didn't want to start the conversation or make something happen because I would be making all of the choices' or my least favorite statement when people are up in front of the class: 'you go first.' By letting the other person 'go first' in life AND class, you're telling the other person you don't want to make any decisions and you want them to drive the conversation and moment. Don't intentionally toss responsibility off onto another person. Is that what you do at work? At home? In your relationships? In your head and your defense, it's probably less about an intentional shirking of responsibilities and more about not wanting to offend another person or take away their choices – or you are just plain stuck. An excess of creativity and choice are just as crippling as limited choices and flexibility. The response to my disdain of the phrase 'you go first' is usually met with 'what if they didn't like the choice I made?' Sure, that happens sometimes. Who cares. Now repeat after me:

Who cares if they don't like it?

This is NOT the same as paying attention to an audience and pivoting to meet them where they are. Remember, you aren't a doormat or a people pleaser. This IS about knowing sometimes people aren't going to be happy with a situation or response. You can't constantly make everyone happy! I'm going to give you another amazing gem of advice – one of my dear friends had this quote on her desk and the moment I saw it, I latched on to it immediately. Highlight, mark this, star it, cut it out, write it on a notecard, tattoo it on your arm.

You can't please everyone. You aren't pizza.

Consider this situation: You're having trouble at work. Your boss expects you to be there three nights a week on top of your usual 40 hours. You're upset, and you keep doing what she asks. You don't understand why she doesn't see how tired you are and how your work is suffering. Next week, same situation. Week after that, same again.

If you never say anything, how will she know you can't keep doing this? You keep showing up, unhappy, overworked, struggling – all just to be pizza.

In efforts to accept your status as not-pizza, you need to do something. There needs to be some kind of catalyst to move things forward. Life isn't just people talking about nothing, or people dancing around a choice – which often happens in improv conversations. People skirt around making a choice by saying things that are just vague enough to keep things crawling in a hamster wheel. They might also talk about stuff – this TV! This hat! These nachos! Or they might talk about people not in the room. It's really easy in life and in improv to talk about things and people that won't respond. Regardless of the situation, this is simply an avoidance of the relationship and reality in front of you.

If 'Becky' or any other random person you bring into a conversation isn't there, she and he can't answer or talk back. It's a lot easier to talk about 'her' than anyone else. In class, this happens ALL THE TIME. Two people will be up in a conversation and they'll start ignoring the relationship and issue in front of them, and start talking about a person who isn't there. I, of course being the kind person I am, tap someone in class and have them head up and be that person that was previously missing. One of two things happen – that person might actually be the catalyst to move the conversation forward, because people finally stop deflecting attention, or, the three of them start talking about ANOTHER person who isn't there – or about stuff. In the second scenario, when stopped and asked 'hey how are you feeling about this?' the response is almost always, 'stuck' or by the blissfully unaware, 'just fine' coupled with their partner saying 'stuck'. The 'just fine' happens when someone hasn't developed self-awareness or is a people pleaser. They are hanging back with the idea of 'fine is ok' and just going about every day with the status quo, or they don't want to offend their partner with the answer of 'stuck'.

Don't be stuck.

If you don't take the risk to say something, your boss will never know you feel overworked and taken advantage of.

Sure, she might not like what you have to say. She also might get really upset. Ask where your dedication is. Challenge how you feel about your job and career. It might get incredibly uncomfortable.

And it might not.

Take the risk to do something or get used to being stuck.

You're reading this book, so you probably aren't that blissfully unaware person who's fine with being stuck. You want something to happen, whether it is an improvement in your personal or professional communication, or a greater understanding of yourself. You might have also recently been that person who didn't take the risk to make a choice. They aren't mutually exclusive. Think: why didn't you take the risk?

In a continuing education class at a local community college, I had two people working through a longer conversation. They were both talking about 'stuff', that common thing that happens when individuals feel uncomfortable talking about and dealing with the relationship in front of them. People talk about that plant or this book or that phone – anything to avoid connection. I stopped the conversation and asked, 'How are you two feeling right now?' and the man, who confessed during his weekly reflection that he had everything he wanted and found that he's funnier than he originally thought, immediately replied, 'Good. It's moving along.' The women, who confessed during her weekly reflection that she had never really stopped to think about what she really wanted out of life said, 'Awkward and like it's not going anywhere.' The two weren't making any real strong choices or taking any risks. We knew they were in a bar, he might have been hitting on her, she was clearly uncomfortable and it was going nowhere. I asked them to start making some big choices, take initiative in the conversation and really define what the relationship between the two of them, along with what they wanted from each other. That *want* should be clear, able to be expressed in a single sentence, and intangible. I didn't want them to aim for the low hanging fruit, like a drink or a sandwich. Rather, I wanted them to try for big picture items like affection or affirmation, something that you have to really work for, and something that can't be obtained with an improvised financial exchange. A sandwich or beer wouldn't cut it this time.

After my coaching, the conversation started going somewhere. He decided he wanted her to make some New Year's Resolutions and she wanted to leave. Once he started fighting for what he wanted, she negotiated an exchange: if she made a resolution, he would leave her alone and she could leave. Suddenly, the whole class leaned in. It became interesting because suddenly, they were both invested and the momentum was finally going forward. He made a choice, taking a risk that she might not want that option. She also made a choice. She didn't like his character and wanted to get out of that current situation. By making those strong choices and taking initiative, we wanted to see more because the two of them were making things happen.

Pull this idea into reality and it all comes down to self-awareness, checking in, and taking risks. In this case, it can be applied to any situation that involves risk-taking or initiative that might lead to an unfavorable outcome. The types of risks and initiative we worry about can be navigated by reading a situation, knowing you either want something different or not, wanting to take a chance, then actively taking the leap. In improv, you don't talk about doing something, you just do it. There's nothing to lose because whatever happens will no longer exist shortly after it happens. In life, we are rarely faced with decisions that are life altering. The two people in the above conversation were hesitant to take initiative because they were both tentative in the risk involved. It might fail! It might get more uncomfortable! Sure, those things might happen – and they won't end or dramatically alter your life.

Say you want to move to a new city. You make the decision to move and you are ready for that risk, so you start looking for a house or apartment. Suddenly, you meet the person of your dreams or get your dream job and it's NOT in the city that you've been planning to move to. Ok, change of plans. You go! Then you break up or lose that job. Ok, now you reset. Start over. Starting over is better than wanting and wondering 'what if?' Failure is never as bad as regret.

Since practice in improv is practice of life in a heightened reality, taking initiative in real life should be easier because it's a bit more understandable and relatable. If you can make a decision in an improv conversation when you are playing a surgeon and there is a dying person in front of you, think of how easy a decision about a meeting or a program or date might be in a reality you are accustomed to, instead of a place of make believe. When you practice taking initiative through improv, when you see that sometimes a choice works and sometimes it doesn't, bolder choices in life become habitual. If you're constantly been avoiding risks in life and you suddenly choose to start taking them, you might initially freeze up. This is where heading to an improv class or doing the activities in this book are key – there is someone else, not just you. What better way to practice getting through moments of inaction than with other people who are doing the exact same thing! Just think: You are in a risk-free environment. Regardless of the risk, the outcome doesn't change your life. You just focus on making choices, not on successes and failures.

Back to the real world, you either make that choice or you do nothing. It's important to note that many things we think are risks are not actually risks at all; they are simply something different than the norm. While different can be uncomfortable, different almost always leads to change. If change is what you want, the move into the different is necessary. I refer, a lot, to choices and risk as 'leaps'. When you take a leap, like a real physical I'm going to jump from one thing to another, you can't half do it. A half leap looks a lot like falling. A risk is like a leap because if you half take it, or half make a choice, chances are it's going to be awkward and weird, and maybe even look like failing to you. You have to do it or don't. You have to take the full risk or be comfortable in the stagnancy. Stop talking about **it**, whatever **it** is. If you want a change, you've clearly developed the self-awareness to know you want something more. Leap.

While improv fosters positive risk-taking, it is still hard for students to take a risk in class. Positive risk taking encompasses the risks that aren't seriously life changing or threatening. Positive risks might be asking for a raise, or talking to your boss about working less. They aren't things like not wearing a seatbelt or drinking super expired milk. Positive risks won't kill you if they go wrong.

You might be sitting there, having never taken an improv class, thinking 'I'm going to sign up for my local class, and I'm going to take all the risks and then taking a risk in real life will be so much easier!' You aren't alone with that thought, and it isn't that easy. Since improv is heightened reality, it's still an extension of our lives and who we are as people. Even if your choice of 'who' is someone that isn't you, it's still a version of YOU. The fears you have, the nervousness, the self-consciousness, all of that comes out and informs that 'who' when you're on the spot. If you have no problem taking small risks, this part of improv is fun. You can take bigger risks and you can think differently about the kind of risks you want to take and how you make choices in life. If you aren't comfortable taking initiative and risks, it's going to make it that much harder when you are faced with an opportunity to take a them, even in a playful situation like an improv class. Define your risk-taking and start small.

Initiative is something that gets easier with practice. It starts with… you guessed it! Self-awareness! Is risk speaking up in a meeting? Is it making a choice where to go for lunch? Maybe where to go after work with friends, because you're always the person that says 'whatever' when asked what they want to do? Maybe it's submitting a resume for a new job, asking for a raise, asking someone out on a date. Whatever it is, you have to know what the word 'risk' means to you.

Try This

Identify what you consider a risk. Make a list of five. Be sure to include things that fall in the 'skydiving' category and things that fall into the 'speaking up in a meeting' category. Examples might include:

Pitching yourself for a job
Zip-lining
Asking someone out on a date
Getting up in front of a room full of people to talk
Sky-diving

Now that you have your five, think about the area of your life that you want to take a risk with first. Unless you want to be more adventurous, eliminate ones that are more 'adventure-seeking' like sky-diving or zip-lining. Now pick one to dissect. Let's consider 'pitching yourself for a job' and think about why this is a risk. Most of the time it's centered on what could go wrong, so identify what outcomes are negative to you, and the probability of those outcomes. For example:

You could not get the job – Possible
You could lose your current job – Not likely
You could never be asked to submit to another job ever again – Nope

After looking at the possible outcomes, the largest probability of a negative outcome lies in not getting the job. Now, address that outcome and think about the components you can control. For example:

You could prep for the moment
You could talk to other people that work in a similar position or at that company
You could make sure your resume and experience are up to date and the best they can be

Now comes the hard part. Do it. Look at all the things that are holding you back from whatever **it** is. Do whatever you can to make this risk as safe as possible; control the things you can and look at your possibilities. Take the leap and the risk. At this point, it's not a blind risk, it's a calculated risk. You've thought about the outcomes, you've prepared for the situation and you've <u>decided</u> to take the risk. In reviewing the risk, if you decide to *not* take it, that's your choice too! Maybe you realize you don't want the job. Or you like your current job. That's ok too! Pick another risk and do the same thing. Take that one, or the next one, or the one after that. Even if it's something like 'eat brussels sprouts today,' take the leap into that risky unknown.

While you can learn how to take risks and initiative, everyone has a different level of risk they are comfortable with. For me, starting a business wasn't a risk. The risk was devoting my time to the business and not having a backup plan. Even though I was unhappy in NYC, it was safe. I pretty much knew what was happening every day – subway problems, weird dates, low on cash. Same thing, every day. It's much easier to do the same thing over and over again than to try something different. When I identified that my life in NYC was making me unhappy and a move to Winston-Salem would help because I would have time, finances and a life, I was terrified. What if it didn't work? What if my business failed in NYC because

I wasn't there? What if no one in North Carolina wanted improv-based professional development?

I was afraid of failing.

Risk is personal. Failure and success are also personal. I'm aware there are specific dictionary definitions of both. Think of a recent success and a recent failure. What were they? Why was the success a success and why was the failure a failure? To most people, failure is simply a mistake. It's something that goes wrong and you look and feel silly for a few moments. And life goes on. Unfortunately, it often becomes this epic thing. We don't want to make that mistake and look silly. There are general successes – a lot of people may think owning a house is a success, or getting married, or having a white picket fence and a dog. Success for me, on this day, is getting through this round of edits and a few months ago it was writing for at least an hour a day. That might mean nothing to some of you. Failure also has some generality. Losing a job, the end of a relationship, not getting something you want – all failures, right? One of the best things that happened to me was a relationship ending, me moving to NYC and then not getting cast in an off-Broadway show that the director assured me I had a part in. At the time? Sobbing failures. Now? Success in disguise. Wouldn't be here without all those tears.

In improv, you're told to play to fail. What does that mean? Traditionally, it's the idea that you do everything at full power and energy because failure doesn't exist. I tell students, if you fail in improv, nothing happens. You get up, dust off, and move on. If a choice doesn't work out in an improv conversation, you deal with the outcome and keep going. The very first activity I do with every single group is 'Zip Zap Zop'. It's the antique workhorse improv activity of all improv activities and there is SO MUCH to be gained from this simple activity. The group stands in a circle and everyone repeats the three commands, Zip, Zap, Zop. They'll repeat these a few times just to get the words in their minds and mouths. Then one person starts, pointing at someone in the circle, making clear eye contact and saying the word Zip. That person looks to someone else, points to them, and says the word Zap. That person looks to another person, points to them, and says the word Zop. That person looks and points to another and starts over on Zip, and the pattern continues.

Simple, right? You'll get this down pretty easily, and you'll probably start off going slow and really thinking about the next word or next person to point to. Happens every time, and every class or group I give the same joke, it's so boring I could die. (NOW YOU KNOW MY SECRETS!) And to you, I say the same thing I say to every single group – now go faster. The element of speed is critical to this activity. You want the pattern to go fast, so fast that people make mistakes because their brain can't keep up. While this activity helps focus, listening, and attention – it's pretty magical with an EE touch. Traditionally this activity is played with 'outs' – the person who makes a mistake has to sit out while the activity continues.

I hate the traditional way this activity is played.

The point of my approach to improv for non-actors isn't to shame a person for taking a risk. It's to encourage habitual positive risk-taking and confidence in taking initiative. If you are part of an improv group and you want to shame a newbie for not being fast enough, by all means. (I hate that too.) The opportunity to give out punishment or to win is not the magic of this activity. When I teach and lead this activity, it's <u>all</u> about failing. If one person makes a mistake – they say Zap instead of Zip, they hesitate, two people say something at the same time, they have a meltdown – whatever the mistake, the whole group makes the mistake. The whole group then puts their hands on their hips, does a hip thrust and loudly says, 'Aaahhhooogah!'

Yup, it's ridiculous. PURPOSELY SO.

Everyone feels silly. You're making a funny noise, you're doing a hip thrust, and most importantly, you own a mistake that might not be yours. You get permission to fail. Everyone laughs, the mood is lightened and people start to think about mistakes as normal things that happen instead of life-altering epic disasters. Mistakes will happen when you take chances, that's a guarantee. If you play everything safe, bad things might still happen. One thing is for certain, if you never try anything new and play everything safe, you'll never fail. You'll also never grow.

If you are constantly trying not to fail, you'll never succeed.

Try This

The time has come to define success and failure. Just like we did earlier for figuring out your 'wants', start by identifying areas of your life. Some suggestions: Career, Health, Relationships/Family, Social/ Fun, Money, Living Situation. Pick one of them and list what you would define as a successful moment and what you would define as failure. Be specific. Don't just say 'Be Happy' for success – what would make you happy and feel successful?

After you've defined your successes and failures, look first at the successes. Why are these successes? What do they have in common? Look next at the failures. Why are these failures? Did you learn anything, or were they dead ends? I'm willing to bet that most of your 'failures' were learning experiences and not life ending mistakes.

Next, think about goals you might have. Revisit the **Want** and **Risk** activities. What outcomes fall under success and what outcomes fall under failure? Now, really think about why you prefer success to failure. Is it because success makes you feel good? It is because failure makes you feel uncomfortable? Why can't they all be seen as learning experiences?

It's important to welcome success. I've spent a lot of time thinking about Ann Friedman's Shine Theory. First coined by Friedman in 2013, it's an idea that folds perfectly into Yes, And. Women, when seeing 'more successful' women, often commit girl on girl crime. That sinking feeling when your friend gets that promotion, date, or attention? That question of why her, why not me? That fear that there is only so much success to go around, and if 'she' succeeds, you wont? The cattiness and jealousy that come out when your friend succeeds and you don't? That's girl on girl crime. Friedman proposes instead of feeling threatened, or seeing the pie of success as finite, we surround ourselves with these amazing women. If they shine, we shine. We all cast our light on one another and make each other brighter.

See how this connects to Yes, And? We can actively affirm and uplift one another. That pie of success? NOT FINITE. Because I'm writing a book doesn't mean you can't too! This also applies to those who shirk away from success, and are afraid to talk about or downplay their success for fear of making others feel bad. Don't be afraid to succeed because you think that someone else won't if you do. And if people are jealous of your success? That's life. We've all felt jealous at one time or another. Check in, own it, and don't let it influence your choices. The people that might say things behind your back? Remember, it's easier to talk about people that aren't there than deal with their own issues. Screw them.

It's go time. It's time to do the things that you fear most. It's time to take the chances and risk making mistakes. I will not say 'everything will be amazing and awesome and of course you'll always succeed!' This isn't that kind of book. What I will do is tell you to fail. Fail grandly. Fail as if you're being paid to fail. After you fail, get up, dust yourself off and get ready to fail again. Failure isn't negative and it shouldn't be feared. It should be embraced. I bet after that last activity, most of your failures are starting to look like learning experiences.

Imagine that one of your 'failures' is a bad public speaking situation. You botched a meeting because you weren't fully prepared and you came off looking like you didn't know anything. Your PowerPoint wouldn't load, you forgot your notes and you kept tripping over all of your words because you were so nervous. It was, by all aspects of your definition, a failure.

Now view this 'failure' as a learning experience. You realized that you didn't prepare, you didn't test your PowerPoint before the meeting and you most definitely didn't warm up your voice beforehand. Next time, instead of fearing the situation, or avoiding similar situations all together, or insisting that you 'can't', you rehearse, test your tech before the meeting and warm up with some tongue twisters. That next meeting? It's so much better because you learned from your 'failures'. While you might make the same mistakes again, or brand new mistakes, you'll also learn to reflect on the situation and grow from all of your mistakes and 'failures'. The more you rewrite your own personal connotation of failure, the more you take every chance to grow into the best version of YOU.

This is the end...or is it? Also Known As, Now What.

You've made it! Either you read the whole thing and tried all of the activities, or you skipped here for the secret sauce that will make you the best you ever.

Sorry. Not here. If you skipped ahead, go back and start at the beginning please. Thanks!

If you made it here after reading and trying the whole thing, you're probably wondering what to do next. As mentioned earlier, all of this improv and improv-based thinking is just like going to the gym – you have to work at it. You can't be your best self with a single class, book, or coaching session. You have to make a commitment to improve yourself and strengthen your skills in order to become the best YOU that you can be.

You don't have to take all of this advice. You are more than welcome to pick and choose, alter and repurpose. I know I'm not pizza, not everyone is going to like me. And I'm ok with that, because my goal isn't to be the best for everyone. My goal is to be the best version of myself, and help you become the best version of YOURSELF.

YOU.

You absolutely are already amazing. Unstoppable, actually. Why? Because you are actively engaged in doing something more than the status quo. You read this book. And if I can help you be just a tiny bit more reflective, self-aware, confident, unapologetic or authentically you? I'm accomplishing my goal.

I have three more things to share with you:

When things get awful, because at times, life will seem like the most difficult place to be in the whole world, remember that you are a badass. Why? You're still fighting. You haven't given up.

Practice doesn't even make you perfect – it makes you better. Keep practicing. Get better for yourself, not for other people.

And remember, go fail epically. If we are all playing to fail and following our fear, we're in the best of company.

AAAHHHOOOGAH! (Hip thrust)

Printed in the United States
By Bookmasters

Printed in the United States
By Bookmasters